I DON'T SEE IT
That Way

To order additional copies of
I Don't See It That Way, by Ken McFarland,
call 1-800-765-6955.

Visit us at
www.reviewandherald.com
for information on other Review and Herald® products.

I DON'T SEE IT
That Way

(It Looks a Little Different
From Up Here)

Ken McFarland

REVIEW AND HERALD® PUBLISHING ASSOCIATION
Since 1861 | www.reviewandherald.com

Published by Review and Herald® Publishing Association, Hagerstown, MD 21741-1119

Review and Herald® titles may be purchased in bulk for educational, business, fund-raising, or sales promotional use. For information, e-mail SpecialMarkets@reviewandherald.com.

The Review and Herald® Publishing Association publishes biblically based materials for spiritual, physical, and mental growth and Christian discipleship.

The author assumes full responsibility for the accuracy of all facts and quotations as cited in this book.

Scripture quotations marked NASB are from the New American Standard Bible, copyright © 1960, 1962, 1963, 1968, 1971, 1972, 1973, 1975, 1977, 1994 by The Lockman Foundation. Used by permission.

Texts credited to NIV are from the *Holy Bible, New International Version*. Copyright © 1973, 1978, 1984, International Bible Society. Used by permission of Zondervan Bible Publishers.

Texts credited to NKJV are from the New King James Version. Copyright © 1979, 1980, 1982 by Thomas Nelson, Inc. Used by permission. All rights reserved.

Scripture quotations marked NLT are taken from the *Holy Bible, New Living Translation*, copyright © 1996. Used by permission of Tyndale House Publishers, Inc., Wheaton, Illinois 60189. All rights reserved.

This book was
Edited by Richard W. Coffen
Copyedited by James Cavil
Designed by Trent Truman
Cover art by 2009 istockphoto/AceCreate
Typeset: Bembo 11/13.25

PRINTED IN U.S.A.

13 12 11 10 09   5 4 3 2 1

Library of Congress Cataloging-in-Publication Data
McFarland, Ken, 1944-   .
   I don't see it that way : it looks a little different from up here / Ken McFarland.
      p. cm.
1. Christian life. 2. Christianity. I. Title.
   BV4501.3.M3335 2009
   248.4—dc22

                        2009009417

ISBN 978-0-8280-2468-6

TO MY CHILDREN,
Lorna, Scott, and Shauna

—AND MY GRANDCHILDREN,
Paul, Ty, Audrey, Max, and
Somebody Awesome on the way.

TO MY SISTER,
Pat André, and my brother-in-law Larry.

YOU'RE MY FAMILY—
and each of you is priceless.

CONTENTS

PREFACE

In this book I share some of the occasional keyboard thinking I've done about how God might see things from His perspective. Make no mistake— God is too great, and His ways are beyond my knowing. I could never presume to know any more of His mind than He has chosen to reveal. But I do know that when I look through *my* lens, it's hopelessly warped with selfishness. When I try to see things more as God must see them, it opens exciting spiritual vistas for me.

What you'll find in the pages ahead are brief observations, insights, and shared personal convictions that are only loosely related but that represent my growing understandings of God, life, the world around me, and the world to come.

Come on inside and sample a page or two or more.

I. REAL-WORLD
Christian Living

WAITING TOO LONG FOR A MIRACLE

Chances are good you've heard the old story, but some stories are worth revisiting:

The town is flooding—the waters rising. A police officer goes house to house to warn people to leave for higher ground—and to offer his cruiser as a ride to safety. At one home, a man answers the door and thanks the officer but says, "I have faith in God, and I trust Him for a miracle. He will save me."

Soon the waters have risen to the man's waist, and a neighbor in a canoe paddles by.

"Climb in," the neighbor urges.

But the man turns down the invitation, claiming, "God will save me."

The waters swiftly rise till they force the man to his rooftop. A helicopter hovers close, and a voice shouts, "Here's a line. Take hold of it, and we'll pull you up."

But again the man refuses. "Go pick up someone else," he shouts back. "God is going to save me."

Finally the water rises over the man's head, and he drowns.

In due course he finds himself in heaven before God. "Why didn't You work a miracle?" he asks. "Why didn't You save me?"

"What more could I do?" God answers. "I sent you a police officer, a canoe, and a helicopter—and you turned them all down."

We can mine plenty of lessons from the tale. The folly of presumption, for one. But for me it highlights that it's vital to understand how God works in our lives.

For example, though He's demonstrated that He can, God doesn't always perform a miraculous healing. Far more often healing comes through the knowledge He's made available that leads to healing—or to avoiding illness in the first place. Some of that knowledge, doctors and other health-care professionals may possess. Some of it is available to any of us if we put forth the effort to find it.

God may not always do something *supernatural* for us when He has given us good minds to learn how to avoid problems or solve them. Having the power to think and to do, we might better focus instead on the *natural* realm of cause and effect, creative problem-solving, and other ways of addressing what life brings us.

And like the man in the flood, is it possible that we are prone to blindness when it comes to seeing that God's *normal* way of helping us is that He's already surrounded us with countless options for solving problems—if only we use what is nearby? God never designed us to sit passively wringing our hands and waiting for a miracle when He has already provided a solution or deliverance if only we proactively use what He's already given us: good judgment, the power of choice, and our own creative effort (a squad car, a canoe, a helicopter?).

We may debate how much God does—and how much we do—when it comes to our personal salvation. And yes, there are some differences when it comes to this area. But my focus here is not on that but on the challenges of daily life: health, finances, relationships, and our personal safety, for example.

Can God work miracles? Clearly He can, has, and does. But how can we ever learn to reason from cause to effect—to understand that actions have consequences—if He unfailingly intervenes to deliver us from negative outcomes? And why should He solve all our problems for us when in nearly all cases He has given us everything we need to do that for ourselves?

Is it not possible that God's greatest miracle is the awesomely powerful and efficient problem-solving mind He created and gave us? Next time life confronts you with rapidly rising water, consider taking the police car or the canoe—or at least the helicopter!

"WHAT I GOTTA DO TO MAKE GOD HAPPY?"

I ran across a forum on the Topix news service the other day—one for church members to discuss things together—and found a thread that began with a post titled "You Better Work Hard to Be Saved!" The discussion began as follows:

"If you receive Christ as your Savior, only your past sins, up to that moment, are forgiven. Now you must get to work to earn your salvation."

It's a good thing the apostle Paul isn't still with us, or he'd be appalled that after nearly 2,000 years the false gospel—the one he wrote the letters to the Galatians and Romans to oppose—is still around. So would Martin Luther.

We *earn* our salvation? Forgiveness only covers *past* sins?

Somebody replied to the above forum post with this:

"What work I gotta do to make God happy?"

Tell you what. If I truly believed this version of the "gospel," I'd toss Christianity in a heartbeat. I'd race to sign up with American Atheists to lend a hand. I'd do what Jo Dee Messina sings about in her song "Bye Bye": I'd floor the accelerator, tear off the rearview mirror, and never look back.

But I'm quite sure my rearview mirror is safe, because if I read my Bible right, I don't earn or work for my salvation—and forgiveness covers not just every sin I ever *have* committed but every sin I ever *will* commit. My salvation was accomplished nearly 2,000 years before I was born.

Yes, I believe that even though I'm 100 percent covered, God won't force salvation on me. In various ways, I can turn it down and still lose out on His gift. But that's something to explore in another post.

"What work I gotta do to make God happy?"—at least happy enough so He will save me? Nothing. Zip. Zilch. Nada.

Slaves and employees work. But Paul and Jesus say we're not slaves—God has made us His sons and daughters instead. He's *already* happy with us.

Picture God smiling as He thinks of you.

WAX LIPS AND "TRUTHINESS"

It's no comfort to me to know that every last one of you reading these words is a liar. Don't be insulted—and, for sure, don't even try to deny it—to me or to yourself. You're a liar—and so am I.

Lying is part of being a sinful, selfish human being. Lying is lurking there from the moment we're born. (And don't try to derail me here into some egghead discussion on the doctrine of original sin.)

My name's Ken—and I'm a liar. And it would take more than a 12-Step Liars Anonymous to cure me.

I remember the first time I lied and knew it. Believe it or not, it took me till the first grade. Down the hill from our church elementary school was a little mom-and-pop corner store. This was long before 7-11s became big business.

We weren't permitted to go down there to buy things during school hours. But one day during recess I walked down there anyway. On my way to school earlier that morning (I lived reasonably close to school), I stopped in and saw something I *had* to have: a pair of bright-red wax lips. They had a little thingie on the back that I could stick in my mouth and bite down on—and then entertain my classmates with my new look.

I don't know where I got the pennies for it, as I don't remember having an allowance at that age. But up on the playground my classmates responded just as I had hoped and dreamed they might—and some good laughs were had by all.

Until, that is, Miss Sparks happened by and asked where I'd gotten my new wax lips.

"I found them on the way to school," I prevaricated.

"Are you sure you didn't get them down at the store?"

"No."

She seemed to buy my lame defense. But my conscience protested immediately and just wouldn't give me a rest. Finally, I edged up to Miss Sparks alone and confessed. I don't recall whether or not she used her "policeman," as she called it (a rubber hose for brief whippings that today would have her behind bars for abuse, I'm sure). But even if she did, it was better to feel the pain externally than internally.

I wish I could say that was the end of my breaking the ninth commandment. Alas, bending, stretching, or even dragging the truth in the mud would recur later in life. The results have ranged from mild to disastrous. Maybe the only good thing I have to say for myself is that when I mess up, my conscience still won't give me a pass till I make it right.

What brought on this reflection on truth and lies? It came to mind as I read of one of those little flaps between presidential candidates during the past presidential campaign. Seems that in a debate they were asked to name their biggest weakness.

One said his biggest weakness was having a powerful response to seeing pain in others. Another said it was impatience to bring change to America. A third, who had actually answered first, made the mistake of taking the question at face value and said something about having a messy desk and not being good at paperwork.

Responding empathetically to others' pain is *weakness?* Being impatient to make positive changes is *weakness?* If the truth hasn't been broken here—at least it's been bent into what host-comedian Stephen Colbert might call "truthiness."

We're all in the same boat down here. Liars through and through. White lies. Black lies. Lies that are laughable. And lies that are lethal.

The only solution for this—and all other evidences of our basic sinful-ness—is the power and pardon of Jesus. *Pardon* for our sins and our sinful-ness—and *power* to change. That change happens as we spend increasing time beholding—and in the company of—the Way, *the Truth,* and the Life.

I'm trying to make that process of change a greater priority than ever.

HE'S THERE—AND HE CARES

This may come as no great revelation, though when immersed in our own set of personal problems, we can sometimes lose sight of it: Every per-son you know or meet—every person on this planet—carries heavy bur-dens. At any given moment, your own load or mine may be heavier or lighter than others around us. But make no mistake—no one is exempt, and no one escapes. Perfect peace hasn't existed on earth since before the tragedy in Eden.

Some problems are right out in the open. A life-threatening disease. A marriage come to grief. Financial desperation. Even these burdens most peo-ple at least try to keep under wraps as much as possible. Then there are the internal problems. Damaged self-worth. Runaway anxiety. Negative emo-tions of fear, resentment, hopelessness, the desire for vengeance.

Sin has turned all of us into damaged goods. We're riddled with selfish-ness. So when our own pain fills our whole horizon and we're tempted to envy those who seem to have not a care in the world, it's time for a reality check. The ultrarich or famous who seem to have it all? Media reports alone should be enough to tell us that many of them battle every day with the dark inner horror that they are unlovable, driving them to anesthetize them-selves from this pain with partying and addictions and a frenzied effort lit-erally to buy happiness by spending.

Most people try bravely to wear a mask to hide from others the weight of their burdens, but behind that facade is worry and pain and struggle.

Someday perfect peace will be restored. Sin will no longer exist. We'll have exciting challenges, but no burdens that steal our peace. Until then, the two things of which I've come to be certain are these:

God is there.

And He cares.

How He chooses to manifest His care in your life or mine, I can't always be sure. Because of issues in the cosmic conflict between good and evil that are beyond even our ability to comprehend in our fallen condition, many of our questions will remain unanswered till we're safely on the other side.

But God knows what weighs on you today. He knows what's going on inside you. And He's not clinical and detached about it. He cares. If He cared enough to give His life to make your eternity possible, He hasn't since then lost interest. He cares mightily.

It would be a mistake, though, for any of us to assume that because God doesn't provide total and immediate deliverance from our problems, He doesn't care. Because He doesn't answer our prayers in exactly the way we ask or by the time we think He should, we can't assume He doesn't care. We can't push-button God.

I've learned that despite what I think God should do for me, I can trust Him in every situation to do *the most wise and loving thing* for me. Even if that may mean He doesn't heal me when I pray for healing. Even if He doesn't rush to refill my bank account when it's perilously low. Even if He doesn't seem to be responding when I ask for Him to spare the life of someone I love.

He is too wise to do for me what I think is right—with my limited view of the future and of what's ultimately best for me. He's too loving, though, to leave me alone with my burdens. I can always have the sure comfort of His being there with me in the middle of a storm.

As a father, I remember vetoing requests of my own children that I knew were not good for them. I knew more than they did and could see more than they could. And I loved them enough not to give them second-best.

If God is there, it means I am not alone.

If God cares, it means unlimited love is at work for me.

Even though till my last breath, I'll have to bear my own set of burdens, God's presence and love will get me through.

ME AND MY TV

As I remember the story I heard a preacher tell, he and his family decided to get rid of the TV. They didn't actually get rid of it, though—just stashed it in the garage.

Pretty soon, along would come a presidential inauguration or a major world disaster—and they would decide to bring it back inside so they could watch the big event and then lug it back out to the garage. But once the "big event" was over, their old favorite shows seemed better than ever, so the TV stayed. Until, that is—smitten with sheepish chagrin—they realized they once again were watching things they really didn't want to see as Christians and once more were wasting huge amounts of time to boot. So again, out to the garage with the TV.

Then came the Olympics, and in came the TV. This time, when the box got its hooks into them again, the preacher cut off the plug-in at the end of the cord—and out again went the TV. The Super Bowl meant that he had to wire the plug back on. A few weeks later, snip—and off went the plug again. Out to the garage. Back in. Ad nauseam.

According to the preacher, when he finally tossed the idiot box into the trash, he said, it had a six-inch cord!

Since my childhood in the "Happy Days" fifties, when every home in my town seemed to have a TV antenna on top to pull in snowy black-and-white images of Jack Benny and Ozzie and Harriet, TV has been in my life too.

I'm thinking now of ditching it. (That's the actual object in question above.)

My reasons are many:

• There's the **content**, of course. It's pretty hard to find much on the tube that comes within miles of Philippians 4:8. Who can argue that today's level of TV violence and immorality isn't a universe apart from *Leave It to Beaver* or even *Bonanza*?

• There's the **noise** factor. TV has become the constant background in most homes. Children grow up never experiencing peace and quiet. They're bombarded with hyperfast images and nonstop babble and bedlam. Constant sensory overload. And we wonder at the epidemic of ADHD even as we fret about the impact of TV violence on our kids. Even we adults need to get reacquainted with the power of quietness in our lives. I'm also insulted when media "experts" tell me that the volume on TV commercials is no louder than the regular programming. I'm routinely blasted out of my chair by the sudden high-decibel screeching of a pitchman with a voice that could drown out a jet engine at five yards and shake loose my dental fillings—sending me scrambling for the remote in search of relief.

• There's the endless **mind conditioning** (a euphemism for what it really is—brainwashing). I'm talking here mainly about commercials—Madison Avenue's ceaseless battle for our minds and, ultimately, our pocketbooks. The primary purpose of TV is not entertainment or even information—it's commerce. A drama or comedy or newscast exists so we'll watch the commercials and part with our money in exchange for some anemic and typically mindless "entertainment." But mind conditioning exists also even in what once was called "news," but which has now largely become propaganda and "info-tainment." Finally, by repeated exposure to today's ever more violent and immoral programming, we're conditioned to see those as less objectionable than they really are. The old Alexander Pope poem I learned in academy is true:

> *"Vice is a monster of so frightful mien,*
> *As to be hated needs but to be seen;*
> *Yet seen too oft, familiar with her face,*
> *We first endure, then pity, then embrace."*

There's the **time** factor. According to the Nielsen ratings people, the average American now watches TV more than four and a half hours a day. That's presumably on top of working full-time. Is it any wonder that in July of 2006 CNN reported on research showing that working parents spend only 19 minutes a day caring for their children? And that "caring for" may not include much real communication at all. People used to read. They used to spend lots of time outdoors. They used to go places and do things together as families. They used to have hobbies. They used to be more physically active. Now, they mostly "veg" in front of the box—content to be hypnotized couch potatoes with passive minds ready to be filled and controlled—their entire world for the moment reduced to a window only 19, 21, or (if plasma-fied) 36 or 48 inches across. I've begun to wonder how much more I could get done if my TV were gone. I don't watch anywhere near the Nielsen four and a half hours daily, but the time I do spend, I'm sure, would make a huge difference if applied more productively.

As I say, I'm thinking of ditching my TV. Cold turkey. Cord and all—no garage. I'd sell it on craigslist or give it to Goodwill. Why haven't I already done it? Well, I'm the kind who tries to think something through before acting. Right now, though, if I were my TV, I'd be wondering about my new foster family.

SUCH AMAZING GRACE!

If I compare myself to some people on this planet—past or present—I come off rather well. I'm no Bin Laden. I'm no corrupt Washington politician. I'm no murderer or drug pusher. I'm no Hitler or Pol Pot or Saddam Hussein or Idi Amin.

Yes, for sure, I've messed up in a lot of ways. But when I compare myself with even some of my friends and acquaintances, I've certainly not done worse than they have.

But this kind of comparison will get me nowhere. The only comparison that matters is how I compare with Jesus. And when I honestly do that, I have to go to the end of the line and stand way behind Paul, who said he was the "chief" of sinners.

When I get a glimpse of just how totally saturated I am with selfishness, it's a wrenching and discouraging revelation. All I can say is, "Thank God for grace!" For grace in the form of pardon and grace in the form of power to change.

"Amazing grace! how sweet the sound," wrote former slave trader John Newton in his famous hymn. Late in his life, no longer able to see, Newton recalled with profound remorse his long-ago involvement with slavery. He spoke to his friend William Wilberforce of the "20,000 ghosts," people he had helped enslave. They had "beautiful African names," he said. "We'd call them with just grunts—noises. We were apes; they were human!"

"I remember," he told Wilberforce, "two things very clearly: I am a great sinner—and Christ is a great Savior." Through his tears a now-sightless Newton declared in the words of his great hymn, "I once was blind—but now I see."

"'Twas grace that taught my heart to fear,
And grace my fears relieved;
How precious did that grace appear
The hour I first believed."

FEAR AND LOVE—OIL AND WATER

This from one day's news: Researchers at Vanderbilt University in Tennessee report that the human brain registers facial expressions of fear faster than any other expression. In their study, smiles took the longest to register.

Seeing a face wearing an expression of fear sends an alarm straight to the amygdala—the part of the brain that cues human beings to potential threats. The researchers theorize that we're wired to pick up on fear cues quickly, as part of our self-protective survival mechanism.

Some—perhaps far too many of us—live our entire lives from a base of fear. Fear of what other people think of us. Fear of loss or death. Fear of not having enough or not being good enough. Fear of failing. Fear of God's anger. And a host of other phobias—fear of heights, fear of tight spaces, fear of spiders and snakes.

When Adam and Eve sinned, God came to visit them in the evening and called out, "Where are you?"

"I heard Your voice," Adam replied. "And I was *afraid.*"

Adam had never been afraid before. But sin is like that. It brings fear. From that moment in the Garden till now, fear has reigned.

Yet even in this life, there is one sure antidote for fear: "There is *no fear in love; but perfect love casts out fear*" (1 John 4:18, NASB).

Fear and love are oil and water. No fear existed before sin. No fear will exist when sin is gone again. And in the meantime, love can cast out fear.

I'm quite certain that in heaven, if we even still have an amygdala inside us, it will have a totally new job to do. Because there hypervigilance in the service of survival will be utterly unnecessary. We will not live under the threat of loss or death.

It will be quite nice to live in a place where smiles register instantly— and facial expressions of fear will be ancient history.

ALWAYS RIGHT, NEVER WRONG— FAST TRACK TO DISASTER

It strikes me that sometimes, we (OK, include "I") can be totally, absolutely, positively sure that we're right . . . and that someone else is wrong. A book about President George W. Bush, for example, is aptly entitled *Dead Certain.*

Being confident is commendable, of course. But being unwilling or unable to admit we could be wrong can have deeply regrettable, even dangerous, consequences. Real confidence is open to all available evidence and, if need be, to making any necessary changes. Self-righteous, adamant stubbornness is not.

And what can be more arrogant than for any human being to claim the certainty of being always and infallibly right? Let's see, isn't there a word for assuming such an attribute of God? Oh, yes . . . *blasphemy.*

Perhaps you've read the following account that supposedly documents a radio conversation between a U.S. naval ship and Canadian authorities off the coast of Newfoundland. It's made the rounds of e-mails and the Internet.

According to the reliable urban legends site Snopes.com, it's fictional. Even so, in an entertaining way, it makes the point that being inflexibly certain of our own "rightness" is no virtue—and in fact can lead to unfortunate outcomes.

Canadians: Please divert your course 15 degrees to the south to avoid a collision.

Americans: Recommend you divert *your* course 15 degrees to the *north* to avoid a collision.

Canadians: Negative. You will have to divert your course 15 degrees to the south to avoid a collision.

Americans: This is the captain of a U.S. Navy ship. I say again, divert YOUR course.

Canadians: No, I say again, you divert YOUR course.

Americans: This is the aircraft carrier U.S.S. *Lincoln*—one of the second-largest ships in the United States fleet. We are accompanied by three destroyers, three cruisers, and numerous support vessels. I DEMAND that you change your course 15 degrees north. I say again, that's one-five degrees north—or countermeasures will be undertaken to ensure the safety of this ship.

Canadians: This is a lighthouse. Your call.

GET OUT OF JAIL FREE

A couple of years back, on one of the major political blogs I frequent, was a news item and video clip of Larry King's final CNN interview of Tammy Faye (Bakker) Messner. The clip was hard to watch. Clearly, Tammy Faye had little time left and, in fact, passed away just a day or two later. As someone who fought my own three-year battle against aggressive cancer sometime back, I have only compassion for her.

Not so, however, some of those who commented on the blog. One reply went as follows: "What a wonderful 'get out of jail free card.' Steal, lie, and abuse people, then pray for forgiveness, and then all is well."

Back in the heyday of the PTL (Praise the Lord) network, Jim and Tammy Faye Bakker did indeed defraud their viewers and covered it up. In addition, Jim's dalliance with his church secretary came to light.

But back to the blog comment. Can we really expect that we can sin—and then get out of jail free simply by sincerely repenting, confessing, and asking for forgiveness?

Yes.

We have God's word on it: "If we confess our sins, he is faithful and just to forgive us our sins and to cleanse us from all unrighteousness" (1 John 1:9). "You will cast all our sins into the depths of the sea" (Micah 7:19, NKJV).

So yes, there isn't a sin we can commit—there is no full lifetime of sin too long—that God can't forgive. To non-Christians this seems like scandal and outrage. People who sin should get what's coming to them. They should pay. They should suffer. And if cancer finally claimed Tammy Faye, she only reaped the bad karma she had sown.

But the good news of the gospel is foolishness and a stumbling block to those who continue to live in rebellion. Yet that good news is certain and straightforward: We *do* get out of jail free. We *don't* have to pay for our sins. The good news gets even better: The penalty for every sin we have ever committed or ever will was paid nearly 2,000 years *before we were even born*. It didn't go unpaid. It's just that we don't have to pay it: Someone else did.

Yes—we DO get out of jail free!

The one who posted the blog comment simply didn't understand that.

REAL CHANGE IS AN INSIDE JOB

I haven't read the book, and I'm quite sure I won't, simply because I have so many other books I want to read that are waaaaay ahead of this one in line. And finding time even for those is a constant battle. I'm not even recommending that anyone read it—though of course some of you may choose to do so.

But I've read a number of reviews and news reports of the book by A. J. Jacobs that soon after its publication rocketed up best seller lists. *The Year of Living Biblically: One Man's Humble Quest to Follow the Bible as Literally as Possible* is the author's chronicle of a year he spent trying to follow all the rules of the Bible as perfectly as possible. Not easy for even the most devout—much less an admittedly nonreligious man.

Jacobs made lists of everything he should do and then devoted eight months to living by Old Testament rules and four months by New Testament strictures.

He gave it his best, trying to comply not only with the major moral requirements (tithing; avoiding lust, coveting, and lying)—but also the "minor" items (he grew a ZZ Top beard, did not mix wool and linen in his clothing, ate crickets, and tried his hand at the 10-string harp).

But he discovered what so many of us who consider ourselves believers have—that when it comes to moral behavior and meeting God's requirements, success is limited when the approach is from the outside in.

The truth is, those of us with strong wills (and that doesn't include all of us!) can in fact positively alter our outward behavior. We can to some extent avoid doing the bad and practice doing the good.

But we can't change what's inside us.

We can't change our inner desires. The best we can achieve is doing what God asks because we think we should or must . . . because we have to

. . . because we fear what may happen if we don't. Unless God changes us, we're rebels.

Only the new birth experience of John 3 can change us inside so that we **want** to do what God asks.

Real change is an inside job.

TO BECOME A CAR, STAND IN A GARAGE?

"A day in the life"—a *Time* magazine cover story tried a while back to profile the "average American" based on statistical averages.

Near the end of the article's second paragraph was this interesting sentence: *"The vast majority of Americans believe in God, and more than 90 percent own a Bible, but only half can name a single Gospel, and 10 percent think Joan of Arc was Noah's wife."*

Unlike, say, air freshener, from which you can benefit simply by being in the same room, just being in the vicinity of a Bible clearly doesn't result in any transfer of the contents.

So 90 percent of Americans own a Bible, but only half can name a single Gospel? It appears that expecting to become spiritual by osmosis or proximity is a forlorn hope.

And kindergarten-to-university Christian education doesn't guarantee spirituality either. Neither does being involved in full-time Christian service—whether as a pastor, church administrator, or teacher.

Even the 12 disciples, after "hanging out" with Jesus for three years, still had huge gaps in their spiritual understanding—until Pentecost, when Jesus moved from being *with* them to being *in* them.

A truism: Food in the cupboard or fridge provides no energy—and never becomes a part of thee—until thou findest a way to get it on the inside of thyself.

Early-twentieth-century American evangelist Billy Sunday once said: "Going to church doesn't make you a Christian, any more than going to a garage makes you an automobile." *(He shoots . . . he scores!)*

Only when the Bible moves from the outside to the inside does it bring spiritual change. Only when Jesus moves from the outside to the inside does He transform lives.

Yes, real change truly IS an inside job.

TWO WOLVES

An elderly Cherokee Native American was teaching his grandchildren about life. He said: "A fight is going on inside me . . . it is a terrible fight, and it is between two wolves. One wolf represents fear, anger, envy, sorrow, regret, greed, arrogance, self-pity, guilt, resentment, inferiority, lies, false pride, superiority, and ego.

"The other stands for joy, peace, love, hope, sharing, serenity, humility, kindness, benevolence, friendship, empathy, generosity, truth, compassion, and faith.

"This same fight is going on inside you and every other person, too."

They thought about this for a minute, and then one child asked his grandfather, "Which wolf will win?"

The old Cherokee simply replied: "The one you feed."

ECHOES OF THE ORIGINAL MILITANT

Maybe it shouldn't really surprise us that there's so much religious militancy in the world. After all, the whole sorry sin mess that we're in began with militant rebellion—with the idea that "I'm right—and you're wrong."

Christiana Amanpour once presented a CNN series entitled *God's Warriors,* in which she explored the militant stance too often assumed in three great religions: Christianity, Judaism, and Islam.

And if believers in a given faith engage in everything from name-calling to bloody wars in attacking those who don't believe as they do, nonbelievers are no less culpable. Such terms as "militant atheism" and "militant agnosticism" exist, too, for a reason.

Militant atheism is the variety that is too often bitter, angry, and contemptuous of anyone so intellectually handicapped as to believe that God exists. Militant agnosticism, not content to hold its own conclusion, takes the presumptuous and condescending stance that "I don't know—and *neither do you.*"

• Whatever happened to tolerance?

• Whatever happened to disagreeing with others without impugning their intellect, honesty, or sincerity?

• Whatever happened to "live and let live"?

• Whatever happened to steering clear of dogmatism and narrow-minded sectarianism?

True, sin is what happened. But does our essential selfishness excuse us to abandon ourselves to smug self-righteousness and arrogant certainty that other viewpoints and beliefs are wrong and that only we and those who agree with us are right?

This—the original and seminal attitude of sin—ultimately leads to our echoing that Luciferian desire to become our own god and lies behind all wars past and present. It's behind the destructive havoc wrought by religious, political, and personal differences—everything from "holy wars" to omnipresent political battles to spouses defending their turf.

People would rather be right than loved. They'd rather be right than have peace. They'd rather be right than ever admit even the possibility they might not be. People seem driven by an essential conviction of personal infallibility—of knowing more, of seeing things more clearly, of having knowledge far more advanced, than anyone else.

I see that attitude in the exclusivity and triumphalism sometimes apparent in the church into which I was baptized. I see it in the condemning intolerance of the Christian Right and the politicians who curry their favor. I see it in the frightening determination of the Muslim world to wipe from the earth any religion but its own.

Though we'll never on this earth be rid of this intolerance and militancy while sin reigns, you have it in your power of choice, as do I, to forswear the deification of our own "rightness" and treat those who differ from us with respect and acceptance.

HEAVEN'S ORGANIZATIONAL FLOWCHART

I read on the Google News Web site that a higher-up in one of the largest corporations in America was fired for violating some policy of the company. His title? Chief information officer.

H'mmm. Isn't that what used to be called public relations director or director of communications? See . . . a *director* is SO yesterday. Now, if you're truly important, you are an *officer*—and a *chief* one at that!

This item got me to thinking about titles. The trend, it seems, is toward ever-more-impressive titles that convey ever-increasing importance.

The big cheese or big wheel at most corporations is now the chief executive officer (CEO). No more of this president or general manager penny-ante stuff. And tailing on to the important title bandwagon, treasurers are now chief financial officers (CFOs)—and mere presidents, a step below the CEO, are chief operating officers (COOs). Even being a vice president is only so-so. If you really matter, you're a *senior* vice president.

I was a veep once in my career. I was in charge of administrivia—of paper shuffling and minutia—responsible for flying about the country to important meetings and attending no less than 18 (yes, count 'em—18) in-house committees that produced minutes (while wasting hours) that referred items back and forth to each other.

Now, maybe I'm making something too big out of all this, but it does seem to me that in the ongoing quest in life to matter, to be somebody, to be in charge of something, things are getting a little out of hand.

It's an old virus . . . as old as Lucifer and his desire to rise higher up the organizational flowchart of heaven to the top—to have the glory and the power. He forgot that true glory and power are found not in controlling others but in serving them.

Jesus said, "So the last will be first, and the first will be last" (Matthew 20:16, NIV). Then He demonstrated those words in His own life: "Let this mind be in you, which was also in Christ Jesus: who, being in the form of God, thought it not robbery to be equal with God: but made himself of no reputation, and took upon him the form of a servant, and was made in the likeness of men: and being found in fashion as a man, he humbled himself, and became obedient unto death, even the death of the cross. Wherefore God also hath highly exalted him, and given him a name which is above every name" (Philippians 2:5-9).

You see, heaven's flowchart is the opposite of ours down here. The servant is at the top. You never rise higher in heaven's estimation than when you stoop low to help another.

Control and power and the most important titles possible? Guess from whence comes that idea? Even the church is not exempt from this pursuit of sounding ever-more-important. A manager becomes a president becomes a CEO. A college becomes a university. Even the janitor becomes a sanitation engineer.

Could we have forgotten that our importance—our value—is found not in titles but in how God sees us? If I'm more important to Jesus than His own life, that should tell me a lot about my true worth and importance—my place in the overall scheme of things.

If I'm to aspire to being chief of something, may it be to join the apostle Paul, who in 1 Timothy 1:15 called himself the chief of sinners. Because with that title, the "perks" are beyond belief: deliverance from certain eternal death; to live eternally with the only one who rightly holds all the power and the glory.

AM I TOO SINFUL FOR GOD TO SAVE?

I'm old enough to remember the old Alka-Seltzer commercials: "Plop, plop, fizz, fizz . . . oh, what a relief it is!"

The good news of the gospel is relief in boldface, all-caps, full-color, digital surround-sound. But I'm convinced that some of us experience only part of the relief to which the gospel entitles us.

We have it down pretty well that we're not saved by being good. That's the legalism that disappears when we really get a handle on "righteousness by faith." Checklist law-keeping or rule-observing doesn't get us into heaven. No amount of church attending, Sabbathkeeping, tithe paying, healthy living, or other good-deed doing gets us in. Neither does any amount of sin avoiding.

Our way in has been paid before we were born—and our ticket in is a free gift.

True, good works such as those cited above will be seen in the lives of those who ultimately walk the streets of gold—but never as the result of an effort to be "good enough to save." No, rather, these virtues will spring naturally from our relationship with Jesus. They will be motivated not by fear of being lost, but by love for the One who saves.

But there's another half to the relief of the gospel that many have difficulty accepting. For if we are not saved by being good, then *neither are we lost by being bad!* But if we accept Jesus as our Savior, He not only lived a life of perfect *goodness* to take the place of any efforts of our own to be good, but also died to cancel out our entire lifetime record of *badness*.

Listen to this: "Christ was treated as we deserve, that we might be treated as He deserves. He was condemned for our sins, in which He had no share, that we might be justified by His righteousness, in which we had no share. He suffered the death which was ours, that we might receive the life which was His" *(The Desire of Ages, p. 25).*

Jesus died our death . . . and in God the Father's eyes, that death erased our record of *badness*. He lived a perfect life . . . and in the Father's eyes, that life becomes our life record of *goodness*.

Do you ever hear voices inside saying things like this?

"You've blown it too often—you've fallen too far and too deep—you've crossed a line so that even God can't fix it."

"God hates sin, and you are one huge sinner. How can you possibly think God can approve of you after what you've done—and what you're still doing?"

Who do you think inspires accusing, condemning, hopeless thoughts such as these? Who has as one of his sorry names "the accuser of the brethren"?

When I was a father of growing children, I could tell you that often enough they did "bad" things. (Though, of course, you must understand that most of the time they were perfect!) Today they're all grown up and have children of their own. Yet even now they still do some things of which I may not always approve. But does that mean I write them off? reject them? get angry with them? give up on them? turn my back on them? quit loving them?

Never!

I'd give up my own life in a heartbeat for any of my children. And I love nowhere nearly as perfectly as does my heavenly Father. Not only that, but I'm a fellow sinner right along with my own children.

So again, we're not saved by being good, and the only logical corollary of that is that we are also not lost by being bad! We can give up any hope of getting into heaven by being good. We can also give up any fear of losing out on heaven because of being bad.

The good news of the gospel is that salvation does not depend on our goodness . . . and is not lost by our badness. Jesus took care of both challenges. And so long as our entire hope is in Him, we can be certain of our salvation.

"And this is the testimony: that God has given us eternal life, and this life is in His Son. He who has the Son has life; he who does not have the Son of God does not have life. These things I have written to you who believe in the name of the Son of God, that *you may know that you have eternal life*" (1 John 5:11-13, NKJV).

TO TRUST WITH TOTAL ABANDON

My reactions to it range from resigned acceptance to disgust to outrage. I'm talking about the pervasive, cynical calculation that motivates nearly every action in this world. I realize that this has been a part of human sinfulness from Eden on down, but that doesn't make it any easier to abide.

It seems that nearly everybody has an agenda. From the moment you wake up each morning, you're bombarded with a din of voices calling out to you, trying to snare your attention. Sometimes it feels as if the onslaught is nonstop. They want to persuade you—usually with the goal of getting you to part with what you've worked hard to earn. They seem intent on winning the battle for your mind—to enlist you in *their* cause, to support *their* opinion or viewpoint, to set aside your own thinking or principles in favor of *theirs*.

To that end perhaps the most effective tactic is to present lies as truth, to hide the real motive of self-interest behind a facade of caring for *your* interests.

The essence of "good" marketing and advertising is to know what motivates people. Not surprisingly, what motivates people is their own self-interest. So every print or Internet ad, TV commercial, or radio spot seeks to make the case that you'll experience a great benefit if only you fork over some cash or credit for the product being promoted or buy into a certain idea or agenda or allegiance. The same applies to the talking heads and pundits of TV news, to the spokespersons and political propagandists of the government, and even to TV preachers.

To cite just one example: "Fair and balanced"? Hardly. "No-spin zone"? Prepare to whirl till you're dizzy. "We're looking out for you"? Sell it somewhere else—I'm not buying.

Little children are marvelous in their ability to trust. We all start out that way. But soon enough, our trust is disappointed. We get burned and let down as we run straight into the reality of human untruthfulness. We learn soon enough to look for the hook, the catch, the attached strings, the fine print that cancels out what the big-print headline promises. And the pain and disappointment we experience make us cautious, wary, suspicious.

Unfortunately, that guardedness and skepticism typically also invade our spiritual life so that we expect God Himself to be no more reliable than the human beings around us. We're afraid to believe that His promises can be relied on—afraid to risk approaching Him with the faith we had as children. Since we live in a world where "if it sounds too good to be true, it probably is," then if—as He routinely does—God, too, says things that sound too good to be true, we're already conditioned to be skeptical.

I don't want to live my life in cynical, doubting, fearful suspicion. I don't want to lose completely the ability to trust with which I came into this world. I also want to stay true to my own code—my own ethics and principles—and not be co-opted into caving to anyone else's self-serving agenda.

To do that, I absolutely must immerse myself enough in the Word to know—and be regularly reminded of—what truth really is. If I do that enough, I can't be bought or sold. I can't be programmed into mindless, robotic responses. I won't sell my convictions on the cheap. And I'll avoid becoming hard and distrusting and cynical. Yes, I'll accept the reality of human dishonesty and deviousness, but I'll stay connected to the Source of pure integrity. And I'll nurture my ability to trust that Source implicitly, even while immersed in a sea of rampant doubt and falsehoods.

When one of my daughters was still a preschooler, I'd place her on a ledge in our house and invite her to jump down into my arms. She'd instantly and fearlessly launch herself into space—with no doubt whatsoever that I'd catch her. Had I not—had I stepped aside—she'd have plunged to the floor with disastrous results. But she knew beyond question that her daddy would catch her.

In a world of suspicious cynicism, I want to be able to take that same leap of faith in trusting my God with total abandon.

WWJD

Among the books I read not long after college and seminary was the classic Christian novel by Charles Sheldon (1857–1946) entitled *In His Steps.* I remember being deeply challenged by its message.

Sheldon's 1896 book grew out of a series of sermons he preached in his Congregationalist church in Topeka, Kansas.

In his novel Sheldon begins with a pastor such as he—Henry Maxwell— preparing his weekly sermon, to be based on 1 Peter 2:21: "For to this you were called, because Christ also suffered for us, leaving us an example, that you should follow His steps" (NKJV).

Maxwell's sermon preparation is interrupted when his doorbell rings, and he finds standing on his porch a homeless man who has lost his job and his wife, and is separated from his daughter. The man wonders if the pastor knows where he can get a job. The preacher tells the homeless man that he's busy—and turns him away.

Soon, however, the homeless man shows up at Maxwell's church and asks to say a few words at the end of the service. He asks the pastor and congregation what they mean when they sing "Jesus, I my cross have taken, all to leave and follow Thee." Why, the man wonders, do so many Christians just ignore the poor? *What,* he wonders, *would Jesus do?*

Shortly after, the man dies in Maxwell's home. The pastor is so deeply moved by the man's simple, honest questions that at the very next worship service Maxwell invites members of his church to volunteer to take a pledge for a year. They are to ask themselves, in every situation of life, "What would Jesus do?" And then they are to carry through on their conclusions, regardless of the cost to themselves.

In the late 1980s some youth pastors in Michigan began putting the "WWJD" ("What Would Jesus Do?") inscription on buttons and bracelets. Young people began wearing these—many of them more as a fashion statement than an expression of personal conviction. The WWJD "movement" mushroomed in the 1990s and continues even today, with Internet sites offering WWJD mugs, rings, bumper stickers, bookmarks, key rings, and other "holy hardware" items.

One thing I doubt Jesus *would* do is commercialize conviction. The evidence of Christ's entire life is that He valued actions far more than words. Words (and that can include visible "statements" we wear as well as promises we make) are too often cheap. Actions, on the other hand, require sacrifice and commitment.

What would Jesus do?

Is this a worthwhile question? I think it can most certainly be—but only if we do three things as we ask it:

1. We pursue the answer in the Word—especially focusing on *what Jesus actually did*—letting what God says overrule what we think. Yes, God has given us great minds, but when it comes to what we truly should do in a given circumstance, our selfish minds—if operating independently of what God says in the Word—can so easily default to a self-serving answer.

2. Once we discover what Jesus *did,* we'll need His Spirit to help us understand what Jesus might do were He here today and facing an issue such as we're facing. What Jesus did *then* will certainly provide the guiding principle for what He would do *now,* and that in turn will help clarify what we too should do.

3. We apply to ourselves what we are convicted Jesus would do, rather than prescribing or trying to impose it on others.

One thing is certain: If we truly did stop often—when faced with a decision or challenging situation—to ask "What would Jesus do?" I suspect that the consequences of carrying out the answer in our lives would be radical and profound.

STRUGGLING TO FORGIVE HIM

Not one of us, as we journey through life, isn't offended, wounded, betrayed, wronged, or targeted for vicious falsehoods by others. I've experienced my share, too.

• I know firsthand how soul-deep the pain goes when others sow lies, attack one's good name, spread false allegations, assume the worst, deny the benefit of the doubt, and see one's truth as lies.

• I have known betrayal by those I thought were friends.

• I've felt the agony of wounds inflicted by those who said they loved me.

• I've known what it is to be vulnerable to someone and feel safe with them, only to be savaged by their rejection or attacks.

From childhood on, I, like everyone else, have been wounded physically, emotionally, and to the very core of my spirit by those who deliberately or unwittingly brought against me their sharp words or hurtful actions.

But I'm not saying this to certify myself for victimhood. I am most assuredly not a victim. I mention these things only to certify myself as being in solidarity with every other living, breathing human being on the planet. For we each and all have been offended—and perhaps even worse, have also offended just as much.

Forgiveness is that highest act of selflessness and grace of which we are capable. And as an editor, let me immediately revise that, for we are not capable of true forgiveness at all—not without divine help—and of that I am certain. I acknowledge your freedom to see it otherwise, but this is my own conviction.

I've found my way, with God's help, to forgive those who have offended me. Even those who have never admitted or acknowledged that they have hurt me. Even those who have hurt me the most. Even those who continue to inflict pain and are likely to go on doing so for as long as breath follows breath.

Just as I am no victim for having been offended, I am no saint for forgiving. It is only the grace of God that has made that possible.

But there is one person I can't forgive—not yet. I haven't yet forgiven the one who has brought me the greatest pain and offended me the most. I have a seminary degree and have spent some years of my career as a pastor. But I am not theologian enough to know how to forgive this person—or even whether God expects me to or can make it happen.

This person is the one who has savaged the relationships of my life. He is the one who has filled my own life with the letter D: disease and divorce and discouragement and doubt and depression and, yes, death. He's the one who took away my father . . . ultimately, everyone else's father, and mother, and spouse, and child, until we're all under the sod. He is the one who makes a wretched playground of misery and loss and war and suffering of Planet Earth.

Yes, you know who he is. I've forgiven many, of much. I have yet to forgive the one who has taken from me the most. At times, I feel waves of purest loathing for him. It's not good for me. It seems to me that I need to find my way to this one last choice of forgiveness.

If that is to be, I'll need all the outside help I can get.

II. A FEW
God-ward Thoughts

ABEYANCE

During the millennium in heaven, I have no doubt as to one thing that will occupy much of God's time. Answering questions.

• Why, God, did You not answer my prayers?

• Why did You let the one I loved die?

• Why did You allow so much injustice, so much misery, so much violence and pain?

• How could You look on as innocent women and children were abused, as Darfur was consumed with starvation and atrocities, as corrupt politicians majored in bloodshed and hypocrisy—and do nothing?

• How could You let the great controversy go on so long?

• Where were You during the Holocaust as 6 million of the people You claimed to love died like animals?

• Why did it seem so often that You were silent—that when we needed You, it was as if we'd been abandoned?

• And why did You let this whole horrific drama get started in the first place?

• When Lucifer rebelled, did You really have to cast him down to this earth? Couldn't You have just banished him to some remote, uninhabited corner of the universe?

Why? Why? Why?

For now, we have to hold all these questions—and so many others—in abeyance. *Abeyance*: a word most dictionaries define as some variation of "temporary suspension."

It's uncomfortable to have our pressing, urgent questions, often arising from great pain or horror, go unanswered. It's grievously difficult to see what we see, hear what we hear, and go through what we experience without the great Why constantly arising from our very core to challenge our faith.

But faith is precisely the key to it all. Holding questions in abeyance until we're safely on the other side is the essence of faith. It's what enabled beleaguered Job to say, "Though He slay me, yet will I trust Him" (Job 13:15, NKJV). Job could not see the full picture. He did not know what was going on behind the scenes in the great cosmic conflict. He didn't understand why the God he loved seemed absent and uncaring while his life fell apart. And the chasm between what Job did know and what he did not know could be bridged only by faith.

It takes not just faith but humility for us to hold our questions (and our conclusions about God) in abeyance until we have complete information. Because that intrinsically assumes we don't and can't know it all. No courtroom trial is complete until all the available evidence has been presented. Only then can the jury reach a decision. And if in fact the hour of God's judgment has come (Revelation 14:7), then we shouldn't be rushing to judgment while, in this life, we're operating with incomplete information—with only partial evidence.

God sees plenty that we don't see. He knows not just the past but also the future. He knows the ultimate consequences of every action, choice, and event. He knows whether present pain will be worth final reward. He knows whether answering your prayer or mine—in just the way and at just the time we wish it—would be the most wise and loving thing He could do for us, or not.

The fact is that if we can discipline ourselves—and have faith enough—to hold our whys in abeyance, someday soon on the other side we'll get all of our questions answered. And when we do, we'll agree with God's decisions. We'll see that if we could have known what He knows, we'd have made exactly the same choices. Till then, we may ask each other why, we may speculate and wonder and try to supply our own answers, but God is the only one who *has* the answers.

True, given our limited information and perspective, it may seem at times as if God is either asleep at the switch or is as caring as an absentee landlord. But how fair is it to judge our Judge when we can't possibly see what He sees or know what He knows?

For now, we have only two choices: To trust God's wisdom and love, based on what we've already learned of it in our lives, or to descend into bitterness and disbelief.

Every single day when I check the news and hear about the abused body of yet another child discovered or when I pray and it's as if the heavens mock me with silence, I struggle to cling to the faith I have. But with time I've concluded that God *does* care about these things—infinitely more than I do—and that He is far more eager than I am to end the misery and get to answering the questions.

Meanwhile, abeyance.

DOPPELGANGER

Ever met your doppelganger? I met mine—twice.

Dictionaries define a doppelganger variously as:

• An evil twin

• A double of a living person

• A person who has the same name as another

Now, most of us have an accurate fix on what we look like. We see the same face and body in the mirror on a regular basis. We have seen our own photos and perhaps videos of ourselves.

None of this, however, prepared me for the afternoon in a northern Washington State town when I looked into the rearview mirror of my car and saw, stepping out of the car behind me—*me!*

Same face. Same body. Exact same hairstyle. Same way of walking. Even the same kind of clothes. A clone. An identical twin. A body double.

He glanced my way. I turned to look at him. Our eyes met. Then he turned, walked to the street corner, and disappeared. I could have followed him (me), but I was simply too stunned.

Billions of people on Planet Earth—and I had just, without warning, met an exact copy of myself. Don't challenge me on this. Do *you* know what you look like? Well, so do I.

Two or three years later, I'm in the waiting room of a transmission shop in the San Francisco Bay Area. They are supposed to be about done servicing my transmission. I'm killing time looking at the cutaway graphic of a transmission on the wall, realizing once again why it's one part of a car I'll never try to fix on my own.

Greasy guy steps to the counter and calls out, "Ken McFarland?"

I open my mouth to answer, and hear the words *"I'm* Ken McFarland."

Only I'm not the one who said the words—they've come from somewhere behind me.

I turn and see a guy who looks nothing like me striding to the counter. Huh?

What are the odds that two Ken McFarlands would just happen to have cars in the same shop at exactly the same time? I mean, neither of us was named John Smith or Joe Jones.

We stopped, looked at each other, did a long double take, and then enjoyed this rare encounter.

Rare, for sure! It had never happened before in all my life and has never happened since.

"They" say that somewhere in this big wide world, each of us has a double—a doppelganger. I feel rather privileged that somehow, I got a chance to meet first my physical doppelganger—and later one of my doppelgangers in name.

But despite these nearly incredible encounters, I fully realize that no one in the world is in fact a duplicate of me. Just as no one is a copy of you. As God made us, we are each unique.

In all the history of this world, there has never been anyone exactly like you. No one on earth at this moment is just like you. And in all remaining history, no one will ever be your duplicate—or mine.

We're as individual as snowflakes. We're a nonrepeatable, irreplaceable, once-in-all-eternity, miraculous creation of God. When life ends and we're gone, we leave a vacuum that can't ever be refilled—a mighty void against the sky.

Celebrate your individuality. Realize that God made you with an absolutely unique combination of traits. Your body, your mind, your temperament, your personality, your preferences, your DNA, your way of seeing things, your fingerprints, your talents, your mannerisms—all are unlike anyone else who has ever lived, is living, or ever will live.

And you and I are not here by accident. God custom-designed us to be who we are. That being true, how can any of us legitimately wish we were someone else? How can any of us question our own value? How can any of us question the value of anyone else?

Yes, I've met my doppelganger in appearance. I've met my doppelganger in name (at least one of them; Google tells me there are a bunch more of us). But I'll never meet my exact clone. God doesn't make clones.

I am me. You are you. As Dr. Seuss said:

"Today you are you,
that is truer than true.
There is no one alive
who is youer than you."

Let's really cut loose and celebrate that!

SUING GOD

Nebraska State Senator Ernie Chambers sued God a couple years back. According to an Associated Press report: "Chambers says in his lawsuit that God has made terroristic threats against the senator and his constituents, inspired fear and caused 'widespread death, destruction and terrorization of millions upon millions of the Earth's inhabitants.'

"The Omaha senator, who skips morning prayers during the legislative session and often criticizes Christians, also says God has caused 'fearsome floods . . . horrendous hurricanes, terrifying tornadoes.'

"He's seeking a permanent injunction against the Almighty."

It's true that it's not always easy to sort things out in this great battle between good and evil—between God and Satan. And sometimes I think Christians do offer simplistic answers to questions that may not be fully answerable until we're all on the other side.

Still, it's also simplistic to ignore that there *are* two sides in this war of all wars and to assume reflexively and unfairly that the blame for all evil belongs on God's doorstep.

We each have to reach our own conclusions, of course. But for me, it makes sense that the devil is quite happy to go around setting fires and then accusing God of arson. From the beginning he's poured plenty of energy into painting God as the villain. For what he himself causes, Satan consistently gives God the blame.

But then, Ernie isn't saying anything insurance companies haven't already said, when they call the acts of Satan "acts of God."

THE ULTIMATE BOTANIST

Sometimes it's just a small news item tucked away pages deep in a newspaper—or in some remote corner of the Internet—that gets me thinking about God. Case in point: "Researchers at the University of Delaware have discovered that when the leaf of a plant is under attack by a pathogen, it can send out an SOS to the roots for help, and the roots will respond by secreting an acid that brings beneficial bacteria to the rescue."

Now, not only is this infinitely cool—that plants have this automatic defense communications system—but no one can tell me that this sophisticated ability developed through evolution. Given the eons and ages that evolution supposedly needs to get anything done, plants would be long extinct before their defense system was up and running.

It's only the reasonable assumption, it seems to me, that the Creator of all living things built this system into the kingdom of plants.

But that's not even the most amazing thing. It strikes me that plants quite likely did not routinely come under attack from pathogens until sin came along. If I'm right about that, then the Creator intervened *after* the entrance of sin, and in a supplemental act of creation gave plants the fighting chance they'd need to survive in a hostile world for thousands of years.

Just thought I'd bring this up, so that next time you see an evergreen forest, enjoy a flower arrangement, or buy fruits and veggies, you'll know whom to thank.

TIME AND ETERNITY—GOD'S ENDLESS "NOW"

So I'm writing a story and at some point my main character hears a knock at the door. I write: "Daniel heard three sharp raps on the door, rose from the sofa, and crossed the room to reach for the knob."

Then I leave my computer, get in my car, and go shopping. Later I get involved in an urgent work project. It's days before I pick up the story again and write: "Daniel opened the door, and there stood . . ."

You see, as I'm writing, I'm "outside" the time world of my characters. In their artificial world, time is linear—one moment follows another. I'm not bound by their time line. Not only that, but for the world I've imagined for them, I know everything that has ever happened to them and everything that ever will. To me, their past is now. So is their future.

Admittedly, this is a limited and imperfect analogy of how God, who inhabits eternity (Isaiah 57:15), relates to those of us here on Planet Earth who inhabit time. And slightly adapted, my opening illustration above is purloined from the great Christian author C. S. Lewis, who wrote a chapter called "Time and Beyond Time" in his book *Mere Christianity*.

When I first read that chapter in my college days, I was profoundly challenged by trying to stretch my mind to understand, at least dimly, the eternity of God. Here's just one mind-expanding (if not mind-blowing) concept Lewis presented: "Suppose God is outside and above the Time-line. In that case, what we call 'tomorrow' is visible to Him in just the same way as what we call 'today.' All the days are 'Now' for Him. He does not remember you doing things yesterday, He simply sees you doing them: because, though you have lost yesterday, He has not. He does not 'foresee' you doing things tomorrow, He simply sees you doing them: because, though tomorrow is not yet there for you, it is for Him."

There's a reason Jesus called Himself by the title "I AM." He did not say, "I was and am." He did not say, "I am and will be." Just "I AM." God is not moving through time, leaving behind a past and moving into the future. God inhabits eternity, from which He can see the infinite past and the infinite future just as clearly and immediately as our "present." Everything is "now" to Him from His viewpoint of eternity.

The implications of this for how God relates to us are profound. Wrote

Lewis again: "God is not hurried along in the Time-stream of this universe any more than an author is hurried along in the imaginary time of his own novel. He has infinite attention to spare for each one of us. He does not have to deal with us in the mass. You are as much alone with Him as if you were the only being He had ever created. When Christ died, He died for you individually just as much as if you had been the only [one] in the world."

Just as I try sometimes to grasp the vastness of distances in the universe, I am nearly staggered by trying to grasp God's eternity. I know I can see only shadows of it with my limited mind here on earth. But someday I hope to explore it with Him in person. Even as I anticipate that encounter, He already knows whether it is to be—and if it is, it's already in His "now."

RC ISN'T A COLA

"It's not PC" isn't about Mac versus PC—rather, PC has come to mean "politically correct." Similarly, "RC" could mean "religiously correct."

Increasingly, the media is all atwitter with the high wisdom—the towering insight—that says it's RC to aggressively and contemptuously dismiss as intellectually and pitiably naive any belief in such utterly outdated ideas as the existence of God or that He supposedly created the universe.

Christopher Hitchens went to bat for these ideas in his book *God Is Not Great: How Religion Poisons Everything.* Hitchens' book has plenty of company: *The God Delusion,* by Richard Dawkins; *God: The Failed Hypothesis—How Science Shows That God Does Not Exist,* by Victor J. Stenger; *The End of Faith: Religion, Terror, and the Future of Reason,* by Sam Harris; and others of like ilk.

Against this tidal wave of doubt and scorn stands the simple statement of Psalm 14:1, NLT: "Only fools say in their hearts, 'There is no God.'" Hitchens et al. would indict as a "fool" anyone credulous enough to cling to the "scientifically proven" anachronism of a real God. The psalmist and Hitchens can't both be right.

At the same time, disdain for the idea of a literal creation is also an increasing staple of the daily news. Creationism, to be made more "PC" for the secular humanist crowd, has morphed into a presumably more palatable version dubbed "Intelligent Design." Both, however, meet with the same derision from those convinced that science solidly supports evolution. In the last presidential election, when three candidates in one of the debates raised their hands in support of belief in creation, TV talking heads found that highly amusing.

Against this tidal wave of doubt and scorn stands the simple statement of Genesis 1:1: "In the beginning God created the heavens and the earth" (NASB). Genesis and the evolutionists can't both be right.

It's my conviction that we who believe in the existence of God—and in His role as Creator of everything—should not be intimidated by those who claim that science and revelation are incompatible. We should not feel intellectually backward because we choose to exercise faith in the conclusions we reach by examining the available evidence. We should not be cowed, as an elephant fearful of a mouse.

I can't *prove* God exists. No one can. While for now we "see through a glass, darkly," we operate on the basis of the *weight of evidence*—not proof. Weighing the evidence is the task each of us faces. And we reach our conclusions individually. For me, the available evidence for God's existence—and for divine creation—is overwhelming.

Three last thoughts:

One, we should give all others the same freedom of choice that God has given us. The atheists and agnostics, the humanists and skeptics—they too get to choose. So we violate the essence of our own faith if we dismiss with contempt the choices of any others.

Second, there has to be a reason for this resurgence of anti-God, anti-creation communication. I'm more than passing suspicious that maybe the devil—whom I also believe literally exists—could be inadvertently signaling the desperation of his end game.

Third, rather than meeting this new wave of skepticism with an arsenal of key texts and denunciations, perhaps we should channel our energies into telling the world what we're *for*—not what we're *against*. Perhaps instead of attempting to dissect and expose error, we should focus on sending our own opposing tsunami of truth to meet and submerge the growing "tidal wave" of doubt.

I have no doubt that God is supremely interested in getting the truth out through anyone who volunteers to be a channel for sharing it. And truth is well able to overcome error.

COLOR ME SKEPTICAL

"A team of biologists and chemicals" the news item promises, "is closing in on bringing nonliving matter to life."

Ohhhhhh-kaaayyyy?

"A lab led by Jack Szostak, a molecular biologist at Harvard Medical School," it continues, "is building simple cell models that can almost be called life."

Almost. I see. But let's read on a little more.

"Szostak's protocells are built from fatty molecules that can trap bits of nucleic acids that contain the source code for replication. Combined with a process that harnesses external energy from the sun or chemical reactions, they *could* form a self-replicating, evolving system that satisfies the conditions of life, but *isn't anything like life on earth now, but might represent life as it began or could exist elsewhere in the universe*" (Alexis Madrigal, "Biologists on the Verge of Creating New Form of Life," *Wired Science*, Sept. 8, 2008; italics supplied; http://blog.wired.com/wiredscience/2008/09/biologists-on-t.html).

So let me review. They're going to bring nonliving matter to life. But it will be life that's *nothing like* the life on earth now. It *could* be self-replicating. It *could* satisfy "the conditions" of life. It *might* represent life as it first began—or as *could* exist elsewhere in the universe.

Sounds kinda "iffy" to me.

Call me not just skeptical, but if you so choose, narrow-minded, myopic, ignorant, or uninformed. But I'm planning to stay by the conviction that real life has only one Source and will never be successfully reproduced by even the most towering of human intellects.

"I am the way, the truth, and the life" (John 14:6), said the One who breathed life into the progenitors of the human race—the only One ever to resume (on His own) living after dying.

I'm staying with Him.

IN SEARCH OF THE GOD PARTICLE

Einstein said that energy equals mass times the speed of light squared ($E=MC^2$). I don't pretend to understand much of the special theory of relativity. But I do "get" that in some way beyond me, energy can transmute into mass and vice versa.

When I read in the Word that God spoke the universe into existence, my own suspicion is that as the Source of infinite energy, God translated some of His energy into mass, in the form of planets and suns, nebulae and constellations and galaxies.

I believe in a God big enough to easily create matter by His creative choice, through thought and words alone, and then to keep it all—quarks, black holes, pulsars, gluons, gravity, supernovae, dark matter, and energy (the whole amazing lot of it)—under His perfect control.

He's big enough to keep the entire universe in perfect order, right down to the smallest atomic and subatomic particles.

During 2008, scientists in Europe began operating the Large Hadron Collider—likely the most ambitious scientific experiment ever.

A massive tubelike underground loop 17 miles in circumference and straddling the French/Swiss border, the collider is designed to fire particles toward each other at near the speed of light, to crash into each other in an effort to re-create conditions a nanosecond after the big bang.

When that happens, scientists hope for something stupendously amazing to happen. As Joel Achenbach, in the *National Geographic* of March 2008, put it, scientists are hoping "to crack the code of the physical world; to figure out what the universe is made of; in other words, to get to the very bottom of things."

The door to the grand theory of everything. The holy grail of physics. The master key that unlocks all doors.

They are hoping to discover the Higgs boson—also called by some the "God particle"—the suspected-but-never-yet-isolated particle that gives mass to all matter. In other words, what makes a table a table instead of a diffuse field of energy—what makes a car a car, or you you, and me me. Or a planet a planet. A universe a universe.

On September 10, 2008, the proton beams were successfully circulated in the main ring of the LHC for the first time. But only nine days later, operations were halted because of a serious problem with a couple of the giant magnets in the collider. This forced the project to a standstill until the spring or summer of 2009. From the outset, some feared that the Hadron's effort would create a black hole that would pull Planet Earth and maybe some of its neighbors inside.

If you're reading these words, you'll know that didn't happen.

Science and religion often circle one another warily, if not getting into outright fisticuffs. Which to me seems strange, since my own view of it is that God is the author of both and that if they seem at odds, they ultimately are not.

Perhaps the apparent incompatibility is simply because we humans are not as knowledgeable as we'd like to think we are—that our view of life and faith and science is so limited that we can't see much of the big picture that God sees.

Even most scientists agree that 95 percent of the contents of the cosmos is invisible to our current methods of detection.

So in my book, 5 percent means we're still in kindergarten. Scientists work to find the "God particle," the key to how the universe works—to how it got here. How *we* got here.

By now, the Hadron project has cost billions. It might have been far cheaper just to accept Genesis 1 and Psalm 33:6 and 9. Like a father watching his child's early discoveries, I think maybe God looks on as we try to make sense of His creation—and smiles.

But would that we here on earth were as eager to find God as to find His particles.

III. THIS ACCELERATING
Treadmill Called Life

WHEN LIFE GETS TO BE A BIT MUCH

Do you have life all figured out yet? If so, please track me down and share. I've been trying to get a handle on it for more decades now than I will admit.

Some days life seems overwhelmingly complex. So many things to do . . . to think about . . . to remember . . . so many people with whom to interact . . . so many emotions that clamor for attention.

Like many others, I'm sure, I try to corral the chaos and complexity with to-do lists, with written goals and plans for reaching them, with trying out the best in personal improvement and productivity and time management ideas I run across.

But even as I sense progress at times, I realize there are whole vast areas of life that surround me—areas with which I have little or no connection. I can check off my personal to-do list, but what about Darfur? I can add to my savings account, but what about wars in Iraq, Afghanistan, and other places? And speaking of places "over there," is growing Islamic power part of Bible prophecy . . . and if so, should I be carving out time to research that for myself?

Am I being a good father, grandfather, or soul companion to the people who matter most in my life? Why is my car still doing the same thing it did before it was supposedly repaired? Should I be taking this new supplement I read about so that I might live longer? Should I dream of some great life adventure such as traveling to Nepal or New Zealand—or should I maybe think instead of helping the homeless nearby?

Life gets so, well, BIG sometimes. How can you take it all in—do it all justice? How can you keep from getting whiplash as your attention veers from here to there?

Since you can't be God and see all that's happening, how can you do a good job of at least prioritizing what's in your sphere of awareness?

Some thoughts:

- I'll never get everything done that I *want* to do in this life—and maybe only part of what I think that I *should* get done. Maybe that's what eternity is for—to keep checking off the to-do list, with forever to get it all done.

• Then again, maybe what's important isn't so much what I *do* as what I *am*. Get the inside right—and the outside takes care of itself?

• Perhaps I could use a little humility in admitting that while I can figure out many things with just the good mind God gave me, I can't always: "O Lord, I know the way of man is not in himself; it is not in man who walks to direct his own steps" (Jeremiah 10:23, NKJV).

• Why else would God say to me, "I will instruct you and teach you in the way you should go; I will guide you with My eye" (Psalm 32:8, NKJV)?

• I think I've decided that if I go through life filled with guilt and regret over the good things that I haven't done, over the bad things that I have—and with anxiety about the future—I'll end up living in a very dark place. I'll try to do all the good I can but realize I'm imperfect and limited. I'll deal with the bad things as Jesus invites me to: through confession, repentance, forgiveness, and starting new again.

• With multiple calls for my time and attention and thoughts, I'll be pulled willy-nilly from this to that to something else till I'm dizzy, unless I have at least one solid anchor—one center post in life to which I stay connected. For that, I have options. Among them: secular humanism, agnosticism, New Age philosophy, or no center post at all. My own choice is the person of Jesus. When I get disoriented trying to navigate the sea of life, He is for me the North Star.

• Finally, I need to accept that life here on earth will never be as simple as it was when I was an infant, when my chief challenge was to eat and sleep. But then, as life has grown more complex, it's also grown more rewarding.

Everybody has a story. Barnes and Noble bookstores and Amazon.com have thousands of biographies for sale. Then there's your story. And mine. The only life you can live is yours—the only life I can live is mine. Let's do our best—and wish each other well!

SLOOOOOOWW DOWN

Are you so worn out that your fatigue is stumbling over your exhaustion? A good many years ago I read a little booklet by Charles E. Hummel called *Tyranny of the Urgent.* He described the frenzied effort so many of us make to "get it all done."

Are you pushed, rushed, stressed, exhausted, hurried, harried, and frazzled? Are you living life on permanent fast-forward? Do you have a certifiable case of hurrymania? Are your days fueled with caffeine and adrenaline?

If so, might I suggest (and I'm preaching to myself here, too . . . why do you think we writers write what we do?) that you take time to smell the roses before you're surrounded by roses and flower arrangements you *can't* smell—if you get my drift.

Check your Bible and see if it still has Mark 6:31 in there: "Come aside . . . and rest a while" (NKJV). Could that be at least as important as "Thou shalt not kill"? In fact, there could be a link between those verses, if you think about it a little.

Sometimes I get to hammering the keyboard at warp speed (ask a Trekkie if you need the definition), and my heartbeat accelerates to keep pace. Then I turn on the magnificent peaceful background of Chuck Wild's *Liquid Mind* meditation music, and I'm slowly carried away to a far more relaxed place. So what if I turn out 200 fewer words that day? I don't want to end up one of those basket cases who need therapy to recover from missing one section of a revolving door.

Years ago I heard one of Danish poet Piet Hein's verses that he called "grooks." He wrote that when he feels fatigued, he gets a craving to "sleep forever and ever" . . . until he realizes that at some point in the future his wish will come true!

Ah, yes. Soon enough, except for the Second Coming, we'll each get our chance at a deep, quiet sleep—not forever (let us fervently hope), but at least until the wake-up trumpet. Still, I rather suspect that managing a little more sleep right now could well defer that more extended rest.

Sure, there's too much to do and not enough time to do it. Always will be. But can we be in danger of so much *doing* that we have no time for *being*?

MY NEXT DISEASE

"So—what is sarcoma?" I asked the doc.

"Well, let's just say that if you were walking in to shop for a disease off the shelf, this isn't one you'd probably want to pick," he replied.

Thus began a nearly four-year journey through surgeries, chemotherapy, radiation, and other assorted medical adventures.

Close to a decade of clean scans has now passed, and I've finally found on the shelf the disease I really *do* want to pick and take to the checkout stand. Frankly, I'd like to contract a terminal case of it.

What I want is *ataraxia*. It's from the Greek word (*atápaktoç*)—and carries such meanings as "peace of mind," "freedom from worry," "emotionally undisturbed," and "tranquil."

To be sure I come down with a roaring good case of ataraxia, I have found that daily injections of Matthew 6:31-34 work better than just about anything else:

"Therefore do not worry, saying, 'What shall we eat?' or 'What shall we drink?' or 'What shall we wear?' For after all these things the Gentiles seek. For your heavenly Father knows that you need all these things. But seek first the kingdom of God and His righteousness, and all these things shall be added to you. Therefore do not worry about tomorrow, for tomorrow will worry about its own things. Sufficient for the day is its own trouble" (NKJV).

As a former black belt in worry, I can tell you a few things I've learned on the subject:

• **Worry never works.** If I worry about the past, that doesn't change what's happened—so worry is a waste of time and energy. If I worry about the future, it never affects the outcome. What does affect the outcome is focusing not on the problem but on possible solutions. Action is worry's worst enemy.

• **Worry paralyzes.** The one thing nearly any problem needs is action. But the action needed is impossible when immobilized with worry. Worry is a set of spinning wheels. Action is traction.

• **Worry is a choice.** So is not worrying. No one forces you to worry—you choose it.

• **Worry is the child of fear.** Ataraxia—or peace of mind—is the child of trust. And trust grows when certain truths of the Word become internal: Psalms 55:22 and 86:7; Isaiah 41:10; Jeremiah 29:11; Philippians 4:19; and 1 John 5:14 are just a few that feed trust.

• **Worry is a hand shadow.** A child's tiny hand held in the light can create huge shadows on the wall—even some scary ones. But most worries about the future really are just shadows. They aren't real, and few of them ever happen. And even that one time out of a hundred that worry steps up to bat and gets a hit, it's usually a weak, pathetic little infield grounder.

When I was a little kid, I worried myself silly when the lights went out. I just *knew* there were bears under my bed—big, angry ones with long fangs, ready to have themselves a little-boy supper. Now in adulthood, I know there never were any bears. So why do I now too often worry about the bears in my future?

You see now why I want to come down with a permanent, incurable case of ataraxia?

LIFE ON FAST-FORWARD

You have only a half-hour lunch break, and you're washing down a protein bar with an energy drink as you push through maddeningly slow city traffic on your way to have your metal-on-metal brakes checked at the repair shop down the street.

Let's see, now—you have a committee meeting at 1:00, a blizzard of phone calls to return, and two carved-in-stone deadlines to meet before you stagger home late with a crammed-full briefcase to a family you hardly see anymore and a house and yard begging for your attention.

Your to-do list is longer than the white pages, you're a walking zombie from lack of sleep, and you haven't had time in ages to balance your checkbook or pay all your past-due bills.

Welcome to the biggest club on earth: the fraternity of the overloaded, the sorority of the stressed-out, the legions of the overwhelmed with *too much to do and not enough time to do it*—the fellowship of those who must *do more and do it faster* just to run in place on a steadily accelerating treadmill. Welcome to a society fueled by caffeine and adrenaline. Welcome to life on permanent fast-forward. Welcome to a world that has forgotten how to stop and smell the roses.

Look around you. Nearly everybody seems to be in a huge rush—walking fast, talking fast, eating fast. People race through the day at breakneck speed, repeatedly pressing elevator call buttons that are already lighted, finishing each other's sentences, impatient with even the fastest computers, multitasking to get more done in less time, driven by what author Charles Hummel called "the tyranny of the urgent."

"Instantaneity rules," writes James Gleick in *Faster: The Acceleration of Just About Everything*. "Instant coffee, instant intimacy, instant replay, and instant gratification."

People are pushed, rushed, stressed, exhausted, hurried, frazzled—and the price is frighteningly high.

In the juggling act between jobs and family, families usually come out second best. Surveys show that working mothers average between 80 and 90 hours of housework, child care, and employment per week. In her *Newsweek* article "Breaking Point" (Mar. 6, 1995), LynNell Hancock quotes a mother of four from LaGrange, Illinois, who muttered, "I'm so tired, my idea of a vacation is a trip to the dentist. I just can't wait to sit in that chair and relax." And fathers too are working more than ever. Says one: "Either I can spend time with my family or support them—not both."

Marriages are strained to the breaking point. Children are increasingly left home to fend for themselves as both parents work—and even when parents are home, they are often so exhausted from overwork that they have little energy left for their children.

In the middle of all this insanity—all this hurrymania, all this frantic, exhausting going and working and doing and buying—God has a better idea. He reminds us that "being" is more important than "doing" or "having." He calls us to "come aside . . . and rest a while" (Mark 6:31, NKJV). He confronts us with our need to recheck our priorities. Is work more important than family? Are things more important than people? Is getting ahead more important than good health?

God invites us to live simpler, more balanced lives. He invites us to slow down and take our cues from the leisurely pace of nature itself. He invites us to step off the frenzied treadmill most of the world is on, to pull over into the slow lane, to make do with less to become rich in the things that really matter.

We have a choice: We can either run with the masses—with the rushing sea of lemmings headed for the cliff to plunge into disaster—or reject the distorted values all around us and take time, make time, for what's really important. Time to sit on a porch and watch the setting sun. Time to read a good book. Time to watch a squirrel hiding a nut. Time to put a puzzle together with the kids. Time to build something special with our spouse. Time to eat right, exercise, and get plenty of rest. Time for vacations and hobbies and volunteering our help. Time to feed our souls. Time to truly live.

Simplicity. Balance. Patience. Rest. Reordered priorities. God's way off of the frenetic treadmill. God's way to health and happiness. God's cure for the stressed and exhausted.

Tyrannized by the urgent? Take back your life. Try God's way. And you'll discover to your wonder and delight that you have all the time you need to do what really needs doing!

PEACE. BE STILL.

When I was a student in academy, I used to hang wall plaques or small posters in my room—or place them on my desk—with verses I discovered and valued as I read my Bible through:

• "And we know that all things work together for good to those who love God, to those who are the called according to His purpose" (Romans 8:28, NKJV). This was the first verse I underlined in my Bible.

• Then I also found a plaque that read: "Paul said: 'This one thing I do'—not 'These 40 things I dabble in.'"

• But the plaque I've been remembering lately said: "In quietness and confidence shall be your strength" (Isaiah 30:15, NKJV).

I tend toward being a rather voluble and outgoing sort by nature. Perhaps even a bit too much so. Abraham Lincoln once said, "Better to remain silent and be thought a fool than to speak out and remove all doubt." But my closest friend has convinced me that, in fact, remaining silent can cause others to suspect that one possesses wisdom worth discovering.

All of the preceding is prologue to one of my ruminations of late: This world has grown far too noisy. And I'd be well served to do my part to reduce that noise pollution.

You pull up to an intersection. Suddenly the earth moves, your body lurches, and your vision blurs as the car next to you—windows down and boom-box speakers blaring—blasts out a wave of pounding rap music loud enough to blow out your eardrums and loosen your teeth.

You're watching TV when they cut to a commercial. Suddenly the volume doubles as yet another high-pressure pitch assaults you with a buzz-saw voice that could cut through hardened steel.

Cities are a cacophony of noise: sirens, jackhammers, car horns, jets screaming overhead, video game hangouts, shouting voices . . .

In suburbia and the countryside, it's leaf blowers, motorcycles, car alarms, lawn mowers, chain saws, and businesses that use PA systems to page employees in the back lot.

According to NoiseOFF: The Coalition Against Noise Pollution, people continuously exposed to noise experience elevated stress levels, mood swings, hypertension, depression, and lost sleep and productivity. In children it results in slowed learning.

But it's not just health that's impacted by too much noise. It takes a toll on us emotionally and mentally—and especially spiritually. How can we really hear the "still small voice" while bombarded with high-decibel bedlam?

If you can get far enough into nature to escape all human-generated noise, it's amazing how basking in the quiet can truly nourish the soul and the senses. You do hear low-level sound: water flowing, birds singing, animals calling, the breeze sweeping through treetops. But it's quiet enough that finally, you can hear your own thoughts. Quiet enough to reflect, to unwind, to relax—and yes, to hear that "still small voice." I have little doubt that part of the enemy's plan is to drown out that voice in a sea of noise.

Some noise we can't escape. But some we can. We can talk less and listen more. We can turn off the TV and listen to peaceful music instead. We can do our best to get into the quietness of nature.

Quietness. Confidence. Strength. Isaiah 30:15 linked them. Try for the first—and see how it affects the others.

CHANGE—REMORSELESS CHANGE

In the mid-1860s, just before leaving on a trip to revisit his childhood home, Mark Twain wrote: "I shall share the fate of many another longing exile who wanders back to his early home to find gray hairs where he expected youth, graves where he looked for firesides, grief where he had pictured joy—everywhere change! remorseless change where he had heedlessly dreamed that desolating Time had stood still!" (San Francisco *Alta California*, Dec. 15, 1866).

Despite his lamentation about "remorseless change," in 1874 Twain was among the first customers to buy a brand-new invention produced that year by the Remington Company—a machine that would radically change communication for more than 100 years—the typewriter.

On December 9, 1874, Mark Twain typed this letter to William Dean Howells (Twain's original spelling preserved): "You needn't answer this; I am only practicing to get three; anothe slip-up there; only practici?ng ti get the hang of the thing. I notice I miss fire & get in a good many unnecessary letters & punctuation marks. I am simply using you for a target to bang at. Blame my cats, but this thing requires genius in order to work it just right."

This was actually Twain's second letter that day. Earlier he'd written a more friendly one to his brother Orion, but by the time he got to writing Howells, he was obviously growing a little testy.

In fact, a few months later, when the Remington Company contacted him about endorsing the machine he had bought, he confessed he had stopped using it, claiming that it was ruining his morals because it made him want to swear. Though he had originally paid $125 for the typewriter, he traded it for a $12 saddle.

Change is inevitable. Once the typewriter had revolutionized communication, businesses had a decision to make: stubbornly cling to the old—the handwritten documents—and fail, or move forward with the new technology and stay current with the times.

Today, typewriters are found primarily in museums or in the hands of nostalgic collectors. New revolutions have overtaken the realm of human communication: the computer, the Internet, satellites, wireless devices. Touch screens are at least partly replacing keyboards. And soon enough, perhaps, all input will move to voice recognition.

Change—remorseless change. Resist or embrace it—but none of us can escape it.

Personally, though I miss many good parts of the past, I welcome certain changes:

• "If anyone is in Christ, he is a new creation; old things have passed away; behold, all things have become new" (2 Corinthians 5:17, NKJV).

• "But we all . . . beholding . . . are changed" (2 Corinthians 3:18).

• "Be . . . transformed by the renewing of your mind" (Romans 12:2).

• And finally: "I saw a new heaven and a new earth. . . . 'Behold, I make all things new'" (Revelation 21:1-5, NKJV).

ARREST THAT CALENDAR FOR SPEEDING!

All of us on the editorial staff of *Insight* magazine abandoned our desks and crowded around a radio somebody had. August 8, 1974. President Richard M. Nixon—only a few miles from where we worked—was resigning his office.

History in the making.

Can somebody please tell me how in thunder it's been well more than three decades since that day? Where, indeed, does time go? Half a lifetime, for crying out loud! From a twenty-something young editor to a somewhat older guy now (OK, so a senior citizen in the "golden years"), I'm amazed at just how rapidly life slips by.

Back then I was a young father. Now I'm a grandfather several times over.

Back then I knew that I'd find a way to change the world. Now I just hope my being here will ultimately have made a modest but positive difference.

Back then I could not possibly know that I'd encounter divorce, cancer, and unexpected career changes down the line. Now I've found the blessings in life's surprises and learned gratitude for second chances, borrowed time, new beginnings, and a new and cherished relationship.

Yes, life is swift and often uncertain. Definitely impossible to script. And even more definitely, brief.

Up ahead, barring the return of the King, I already see a finish line in the distance growing closer. So what advice do I have for my descendants and all those newer to this earth than I am? Basically, three things.

• Make your moments really count and be profusely and profoundly grateful for every one of them.

• Give away to others—with reckless abandon—all the love and affirmation you possibly can.

• And de-invest in this short life—build your portfolio for the next one.

IV. NO ONE
Is an Island

THE RIPPLE EFFECT

In an episode of the 1960s TV series *Star Trek*, Captain James T. Kirk of the spaceship *Enterprise* and his crew travel back in time to pre-World War II America. Kirk falls in love with a young woman who, as determined by science officer Spock, is destined to directly affect the course of the immediate future. She will either go on to lead a successful pacifist movement in the United States, which will delay its entry into the conflict and thus make it possible for Nazi Germany to win the war—or she will die in a traffic accident.

One evening, Kirk, Spock, and Dr. Leonard McCoy meet on a town sidewalk. Across the street, the young woman sees them and begins to cross over to meet with them, but she doesn't see the large truck speeding toward her. Dr. McCoy rushes to push her clear of danger, but Kirk—knowing the outcome should she live—restrains McCoy, and the young woman dies.

A recurring conundrum of time-travel stories centers on what happens when a person who travels back in time interferes with an event, thereby setting in motion a ripple effect of changes that can amplify till it changes the entire outcome of history.

Whatever the dilemmas posed by science-fiction writers, it is no theory that every person alive influences others. Sometimes that influence is only slight or temporary—sometimes it is lasting and profound. Every one of us knows of people whose influence on us has been powerful, perhaps changing the entire course of our lives. Truly no one is an island. We all affect those around us.

You'll be meeting, working with, calling, e-mailing, texting, encountering who knows how many people today. So will I. Let's try today to be mindful of the impact we'll have on those around us.

Let's try to remember that we *can* make a difference. We can encourage or discourage. We can bring uplift or put down. We can share positivity or negativity. We can perhaps say, do, or model something that will change the course of someone's life.

All this and more is within our power.

We can choose it—and make it happen.

"I ONLY HAVE TWO DOLLARS"

If I live out my biblical "three score and ten" (70 years), that means I'm here on earth for about 25,550 days. Now, I'm hoping to manage at least 80 years (29,200 days) or even 90 (32,850).

And while I have no guarantees (and neither do you) of even one more day, much less a full 70, 80, or 90 years, I began to ponder my remaining time. What do I still hope to get done? What do I need to do to make those things happen? What's really important?

Later that day, I ran across one of John Wesley's sayings:

"Do all the good you can,
By all the means you can,
In all the ways you can,
In all the places you can,
At all the times you can,
To all the people you can,
As long as ever you can."

H'mmmm. Time in limited supply. But do good as long as ever I can? Where do I crowd in all this "do-gooding" when my own to-do list is already hopelessly long?

Before the day was out, I had at least part of the answer. Rushing out to do some errands, I stopped at a store and ran in to grab a couple of items.

Returning to my car, I settled in, turned the ignition, and on came the welcome flow of air conditioning. It was slowly cooling into autumn, but where I live, temps were still in triple digits.

That's when I saw her.

A little girl—maybe 8 or 9—was striding toward me with purpose showing in her eyes. I could tell she had every intention of tapping on my car window, so I powered it down, expecting her pitch for some pocket change.

"My mama would like to give you two dollars," she said, "if you could drive us back home."

I followed her pointing arm . . . and maybe 50 feet away, sitting on a curb, was a young and very pregnant Hispanic mother with four other "stairsteps"—ranging from toddlers to the oldest one standing at my window. Five—and one on the way.

I was truly in a hurry, but it was *so* hot outside, and the mother looked exhausted. I have an older, 1990s-vintage car, but it's roomy. We got every-body in, along with the box containing a new stroller the mother had bought at a discount store nearby and some little bottles of water.

I turned the air-conditioning on full blast, and the mama did navigation as I drove two, maybe three, miles.

"Did you *walk* to the store?" I asked.

"Yes," she replied wearily. I could barely imagine that little tribe walk-ing so far in the heat.

"I only have two dollars," she said as we approached her older apartment building.

"You keep it," I said. "I have a few kids myself, and I remember those days when they were little."

The mother and her kiddos thanked me profusely as they piled out and headed for their unit. Amazingly courteous kids!

I drove away, not proud even one molecule for my act of helping. Instead, the day all began to come together as a light went on inside.

Do all the good I can . . .

How many opportunities might I have lost already—just by being too rushed or unobservant? And if I were to remember this day, how many op-portunities might I still find?

No matter how many days I have remaining . . . I'd like to get to the end of the line and realize that on a hot summer day something happened late in the game to wake me up to at least part of why I was put here in the first place.

SEEING THROUGH NEW EYES

Some time ago I watched a particular episode of the TV medical drama *House*. In the series, actor Hugh Laurie plays Dr. Gregory House—a crotch-ety doc seemingly devoid of bedside manner but a brilliant diagnostician nonetheless.

In the episode entitled "Human Error" Dr. House tells a husband that his wife is technically dead and being kept alive only by machine assistance. The time has come, House advises, to let her go.

The machine is shut down, and the husband sobs as he leans across his wife, embracing her as he tells her a final goodbye. Suddenly he feels her heart beating—on its own. Long story short: she lives, and Dr. House dis-covers and corrects the rare heart condition that caused her apparent death.

In the scene in which the husband tells his wife goodbye, it struck me again—as it has countless times during my life—how priceless is the value of a single human life. It's through personal loss and not just fictional drama, of course, that this point gets repeatedly driven home.

Our God, thankfully, never loses sight of the value of life. He is the one who gave it and is its source. And He never loses sight of the value of each person. He is the reason each of us is here. He is the one who died for us personally—individually.

But sometimes we don't seem to value each other much. So often even those who lose a spouse, child, parent, or other loved one in death wish afterward with regret that they had treated their loved one better. If only . . .

As I've traveled through life, some people haven't rated very high in my estimation. Some I've had very negative thoughts and feelings about. I've resented people. I've been angry with people. And some I've felt genuine contempt for (somehow politicians often end up on this list of mine).

These attitudes of mine are wrong, I freely admit. And I routinely have to confess and repent as I bring these things to God.

Suppose I come across someone I just can't stand and find that person trapped in a burning car. I'm quite certain that even if I recognized them, I'd do all I could to get them out. So maybe I too value human life.

If so, why can't I also value the worth, the individuality, of every person I meet, know, or even hear about? Someone in his family—perhaps his daughters—doubtless grieved when Saddam Hussein died. He mattered to them. He also mattered to God, who gave him life and died so that the dictator could have the chance to live forever.

Some people seem just plain evil. Some have personalities that grate like nails on a chalkboard. Some are so arrogant and full of themselves it's nauseating. Some go out of their way to hurt and lie about other people. Some seem riddled with bigotry . . . with hostility toward anyone not exactly like themselves.

But the fact remains that every person I—we—despise or even just dislike remains precious to somebody. Through somebody's eyes that person is priceless and quite wonderful.

That's how God sees each of us.

And how God sees me (despite my flaws) is how I need to see others . . . and wish I did. But it will never happen as long as I see them through my own sinful and selfish eyes (eye trouble that is really "I" trouble).

I need to see others (as Amy Grant sings in "Father's Eyes") as God the Father sees them.

THE HAVES—AND THE HAVE-NOTS

In Mexico City a few years ago I had some time between meetings there to explore various parts of the megalopolis. In many areas of the city I saw slums filled with miserable hovels: "homes" made of cardboard, sheet metal, discarded planks, ragged blankets. Yet other parts of town contained massive, grand mansions.

Even here in America, the contrast between the haves and the have-nots is staggering. Most large cities have their slums, ghettos, and shantytowns— but also their gated luxury estates. And the gap between the wealthiest and the poorest widens both in the United States and around the world. Consider these statistics, accurate as of late 2008:

• Nearly half of the world's people live on less than $2 a day. Of those, about a billion live on less than $1 a day.

• The world's three richest people are wealthier than the world's poorest 48 nations (a quarter of the world's countries).

• The slice of the world's total wealth taken by the richest 1 percent is the same size as that handed to the poorest 57 percent.

• The world's nearly 1,000 billionaires have a combined wealth greater than that of the poorest half of humanity.

• Number of children in the world: 2.2 billion. Number of them living in poverty: 1 billion.

• The richest 1 percent of adults owns 40 percent of the world's total assets. The richest 10 percent of adults account for 85 percent of total assets. The bottom half of the world adult population owns 1 percent of global wealth.

• The top 1 percent of Americans receives more income than the bottom 40 percent.

• The poorest one fifth of the U.S. population receives less than 4 percent of the total income. The richest one fifth receives more than 50 percent.

The uneven distribution of wealth in our world is yet another symptom of what happens when selfishness becomes the fundamental driving principle of life here on earth. To Satan I ask, "Was this how it was in heaven before you rebelled? Is this what happens when you are in charge? Is this the best you have to offer?"

Before sin, *everyone* was wealthy! There were only haves—no have-nots. But now, most people of the world live in misery and starvation, while a few live lives of unimaginable wealth and ease.

My thoughts about this tragic reality?

1. No matter how tough things get for me, if I'm living on more than $2 a day I'm in the "rich half" of the world's population.

2. I can't right the gross inequities in this world. But maybe I can right a few—or one. The more I let go of "get" and embrace "give," the happier my life will be.

3. Railing against greedy individuals and demanding that they share more of their wealth is pointless. Genuine altruism and generosity must come from within.

4. What can I do to redress this imbalance? Perhaps not much in tangible terms. But I can help point both poor and wealthy to the only One who can provide what they each need.

On my Mexico City trip the street beggars were everywhere—just as in some American cities, panhandlers seem to be at every freeway off-ramp stoplight. I'm not one given to filling every outstretched hand. But one evening in the Zona Rosa of Mexico City a ragged, weary father stood in the shadows, silent tears sliding down his face, as he held his clearly ill little boy in his arms. Our eyes met. I opened my wallet and found the largest denomination of Mexican currency I had—and slipped it into his hand.

No, we can't fix it all. And sometimes the overwhelming need around us breaks the heart. But we *can* do some small thing.

Tomorrow perhaps a good check will come to me, and I'll make a donation or help a friend. For today, I'm writing these words and inviting you to put something, however small, into the yawning chasm of the world's need.

TREATING PEOPLE "AS IF"

It's fairly easy to treat people the way they deserve to be treated. In fact, most of the time when people mess up—when they really blow it—it's just a given that they should get what they have coming.

I certainly can't endorse the personal failings and shenanigans of people in public life—politicians, Hollywood stars, sports heroes—whose sins and crimes routinely come to light. I can't approve of the actions of church leaders—even lay Christians—who rail against the very sins in which they are sometimes discovered to be involved.

But I'm truly far more troubled by the predictable reaction of so many who rush to bring down judgment and condemnation when someone steps outside the lines. After all, say the stone throwers, people have to learn that actions have consequences, right? They need to be "taught a lesson." They need to be "made an example." They need to "pay for what they've done." They should have "known better."

I'm troubled by the gleeful and smug satisfaction so often evidenced when someone falls or fails—even when such people bring it on themselves. It's as if those who— for the moment, at least— haven't yet themselves been "caught" or "accused," or even just "suspected," live above all such human weaknesses.

But God says we've *all* sinned and come short. So it ill-behooves any of us to nurture the illusion that we're one whit better than anyone else. Looking at the sins others commit, we'd like to think that *our* sins are far less objectionable than theirs are. But we're *all* on death row. What room do we have to condemn those in the cells on either side of us?

I can't begin to tell you what an ongoing relief it is to know that God doesn't treat people as they deserve—He treats them "as if."

The little book *Steps to Christ* says, "If you give yourself to [Jesus], and accept Him as your Savior, then, sinful as your life may have been, for His sake you are accounted righteous. Christ's character stands in place of your character, and you are accepted before God just *as if* you had not sinned" (p. 62; italics supplied).

And though I couldn't possibly recommend everything he ever wrote, the great German writer Johann Wolfgang von Goethe once said: "Treat people as if they were what they ought to be, and you help them to become what they are capable of becoming."

Imagine how applying that principle affects children! If we treat them as if they are unimportant, valueless, to be seen only but not heard, as always wrong, as "bad"—then that's the hopeless, discouraging image of themselves they will develop. They will surely meet our low expectations for them.

On the other hand, if we treat them as priceless, as important, as filled with limitless potential—if we teach them that failing is simply a normal and valued part of learning—then they will see themselves as the magnificent creations of God whom they truly are.

I'm so everlastingly grateful that God does not treat me as I deserve. If He did, I'd be utterly without hope. Instead, He treats me "as if" I had never sinned! Incredibly, He treats me "as if" my sins and failures never happened. He isn't in the business of condemning me and raining down judgments. He's in the business of forgiving and restoring and redeeming me.

"There is therefore now *no condemnation* to them which are in Christ Jesus" (Romans 8:1).

"For God sent *not* his Son into the world *to condemn* the world; but that the world through him might be saved" (John 3:17).

And if God isn't in the business of judging and condemning *me,* how dare I judge or condemn anyone else? "*Judge not,* and you shall not be judged. *Condemn not,* and you shall not be condemned. *Forgive,* and you will be forgiven" (Luke 6:37, NKJV).

The golden rule is really my simply treating other people "as if" they were me—as I'd want them to treat me—with mercy and forgiveness and even "the benefit of the doubt" and not with judgment and condemnation and a long memory of their offenses. The golden rule means my helping to cover from view the sins of others—not exposing the wrongdoing and humiliating them.

Thank God that He ultimately applies justice only to those who ultimately reject mercy. As for me, I'm planning to take hold of God's mercy so tightly every day that it's "as if" it's been surgically attached!

V. MUSINGS OF AN
Amateur Theologian

THE GOOD NEWS FIGHT

Three couch potatoes sprawled across the living room furniture one evening in front of the TV when their favorite program—*CSI: Topeka*—was suddenly interrupted by that laundry-detergent commercial starring the Mud Puddle Kid.

Up on the screen, a weary mother looked blissfully grateful for the box of Mud-B-Gone detergent she hugged tightly in her arms, as—out in the street in front of the house—her young son stomped gleefully through the muddy puddles in his freshly laundered pants.

"Would you look at that?" remarked Couch Potato 1. "That kid has messed up his spanking-clean clothes with that yucky mud. Good thing his mom has that detergent."

"Well, maybe," added Couch Potato 2, "but what good does it do for her to wash his clothes if all he does is run right back out and stomp through the puddles again? What this kid needs is for somebody to make it so that he doesn't even *want* to stomp in puddles again."

Up on the TV screen, the Mud Puddle Kid continued to drench himself in muddy goo, as Couch Potato 3 put in his two cents' worth. "It's one thing to clean up the kid when he gets muddy," he said. "And it's another to fix it so he doesn't even want to get muddy. But what would *really* solve everything is if somebody could take away the mud puddles themselves. Now, *that* would truly be good news!"

It pains me to say it, but the three couch potatoes got into such an argument over who had the right solution that they ended up out in the street in front of their own house, slinging mud at each other.

Sad to say, Christians sometimes get into the same kind of argument about the good news of salvation. Some say that when we get all covered with the mud of sin, we need God to forgive us and clean us up. Others say that this doesn't do much good unless somehow God can do something about our desire to keep sinning. And finally, some say that we can never be fully saved from sin until God takes sin itself away.

The truly good news is that ultimately God delivers us from sin's *penalty, power,* and *presence.*

Each spud saw only part of that truth—though of course all three of them were right!

TRUTH IS LIKE A CAMCORDER

I already have a pretty decent digital camera. Having about a half dozen of the planet's most irresistible grandkids in my downline, I jolly well better have!

Now, some people have *technophobia*—a fear of all things high-tech and gadget-like. I'm one of many plagued with the opposite: *technophilia*, which I define as a strong enthusiasm for technology, especially the latest that brims with all kinds of must-have new and better features.

Thus, few days pass in which I don't spend at least part of my daily thinking quota on all the good reasons I *need* a camcorder. More specifically, I *need* a hi-def camcorder with a 48x optical zoom and enough bells and whistles to dazzle even a nontechie.

Obviously, the astonishingly fast change and growth rate of my grand-descendants seems a pressing and legitimate part of the argument.

As I've pondered (that too seems to be one of my enthusiasms—pondering stuff), it seems to me that truth is a lot more like a camcorder than a digital still camera. The latter freezes the action in its tracks, even if the action includes closed eyes or strange facial expressions. The former, on the other hand, "unfreezes" the action and shows a segment of life more as it actually happens: fluid, dynamic, ever-changing.

I happen to believe that such a thing as ultimate, objective truth exists. I don't (for now, at least) believe that God has endless gazillions of variations on truth, any one of which is just peachy.

Of course, God has a challenge getting His truth through to us in ways that we can understand. First of all, His mind is so far beyond ours that even to compare it with, say, my earnestly trying to explain all I know about nuclear fission to a passing bug, is not an adequate comparison. The gap is far greater between my mind and God's.

Not only is God's mind so beyond ours that He truly must have expended some major energy just trying to find a way to communicate His truth in our language—He had only sin-impaired people through whom to send it. The Bible writers were riddled with the sin virus and all that the selfishness disease has done to the human ability to reason accurately. Bible writers also came with the baggage of their own preconceptions, literary in-adequacies, and cultural viewpoints.

Nonetheless, God did the best He could with what He had. And that was only in Phase I: getting the truth in print. Then came Phase II: the challenge of those who would *read* His messages. If anything, the readers were far worse off than had been the writers.

Even if you factor in that God through the Holy Spirit kept His hand closely over the whole process from beginning to end, given the challenges already mentioned, the chances for misunderstanding, misinterpretation, and deliberate "wresting," as the Word says, were—and are—high.

The result can be seen in the *World Christian Encyclopedia*'s research re-porting at least 10,000 distinct religions worldwide, of which Christianity is only one. Within Christianity itself, a further division results in 33,830 de-nominations. And guess what? Do you think anyone belongs to any of those religions, groups, denominations, who does not believe that it has "the truth"?

I would not want to suggest or imply that because of all these various conceptions of it, truth therefore isn't possible to know. I'm not ready to jump ship and sign on with agnosticism. In fact, I'd go even further than the encyclopedia and say that no two people on the planet see or understand truth exactly the same.

And maybe that's not all a bad thing. Maybe that means that God does have ultimate, unchanging truth out there but that He knows He made each of us to be unique. As such, not only are our brains uniquely wired, but our personalities, gender-influenced perspectives, temperaments, life experiences and environments, childhood upbringing, emotions, thought patterns, brain chemistry, hormone balances, DNA—and all else that makes each of us who we are—is as individual as the snowflakes that fall.

Maybe God knows what truth *I* need most to get straight—and I can count on Him to reveal that to me according to *His* priorities and time schedule. If so, then maybe He's speaking truth to me that may not be on His calendar for you till years from now—if ever. Or the reverse may be true.

Now, what about this camcorder versus digicam business?

Well, just as I suspect, God progressively reveals His truth to me on His own personalized schedule, I think He does the same in how He shares truth with His church—His "body" on earth. If so, that has implications. Such as:

While truth itself may have only one full and ultimate version, as God has set it up, our *understanding* of truth may well be (and I believe should be) progressive. If so, then we do well to be in a constant mode of open-mindedness—of eager readiness to revise our understanding as God brings us His steadily unfolding revelation of any given truth.

And if this is how God reveals truth, what happens when we make the mistake old Israel did and freeze truth into a systematized, dogmatic, set-in-cement creed that never changes? Does that not frustrate God's purpose and plan? And does it not utterly truncate His "word" of truth in midsentence, risking erroneous conclusions and possibly tragic consequences?

I'm reminded of what happened at Napoleon's Battle of Waterloo in 1815, where an Anglo-allied force under the Duke of Wellington came against him. The message that came through in Britain on June 18, 1815, from Winchester Cathedral, spelled out in code, "W-E-L-L-I-N-G-T-O-N D-E-F-E-A-T-E-D"—and at that point, the fog closed in and the message light could no longer be seen. Great despair followed the message, till the fog suddenly lifted, and the full message could now be seen: "W-E-L-L-I-N-G-T-O-N D-E-F-E-A-T-E-D *T-H-E E-N-E-M-Y.*"

When we latch onto truth and then close ourselves to even the possibility that we might have interrupted God in midsentence—that He might not be done yet—we take a great risk. We make ourselves vulnerable to the same rigidity, authoritarianism, dogmatism, and self-righteous but unjustified certainty that befell ancient Israel. God may indeed have His end-time incarnation of His original chosen people—Israel II, if you will—but it too is at risk for repeating that same mistake.

Am I saying that because God's revelation of truth—and our understanding of it—is progressive, truth itself is constantly in flux, and that indeed there IS no ultimate truth? Not at all! No more than the reality of a scene from life changes simply because a camcorder reveals more of it with each minute recorded. If I'm using my future camcorder to record one of my "world's most awesome" grandchildren, does the view ever stay the same? Not for a second! But does that mean there is no such thing, ultimately, as my grandchild? You'll never sell *me* that!

Since my earliest exposure to spiritual truth, my understanding of any given facet of it has changed . . . sometimes only incrementally, sometimes dramatically. I don't understand the truths of the Second Coming, the Sabbath, or how salvation works in just the way I did when I was a child—or a young man. That *would* be the case, of course, if I had taken my first understanding of truth, shot a still camera photo of it, and chosen to believe that it was now locked in, nevermore to change. Oh, were that only true of the photos of *me* from earlier in life!

No, I've found that by rejecting dogmatism and staying wide open to whatever God has to show me, my understanding of truth has shifted, changed, and expanded. And that process won't end for as long as I draw breath.

Does that mean "ultimate, objective truth" does not exist? No, not as I see it, anyway. But again, both God's revelation of truth and especially my understanding of it are progressive.

I look forward to arriving in heaven not long hence, not to pick up my diploma, but to enter a never-ending grad school in which I'll never finish learning more and more and more about God and His truth!

And just as a camcorder beats a still camera hands down, whatever way God has waiting by which to show me more, it will put even my fervently desired supercamcorder in the shade!

CHRIST IN YOU—YOU IN CHRIST

Whether you call it the "plan of salvation" or "righteousness by faith," the topic of how God saves us from sin often seems impossibly complicated.

Sometimes you read the hairsplitting and pretentious pontificating of theologians, and you're left with the impression that unless you have a doctorate or two and live in an ivory tower, you're simply not equipped to understand redemption (or *soteriology,* as they would more likely put it).

Yet if salvation isn't simple enough for even a child to understand, then God hasn't reached down far enough to save everyone.

In my own church, the topic—usually flying under the flag "righteousness by faith"—has divided churches, pitted members against each other, often generated more heat than light, and, like an autoimmune disease, has caused the body of Christ to declare war on itself.

Perhaps a large part of the problem is simply that we too often yield to the natural selfish human impulse to speak and debate and contend more than we listen and pray and seek. Because the truth in all its simplicity is right there in the Word—and the Spirit of God is not just available but eager to make it unmistakably clear.

An old preacher supposedly said, "When I was young, I had all Bible truth comprised in 300 doctrines. Now that I'm old, I have only two: 'I am a great sinner'—and 'Jesus is a great Savior.'"

I believe the old cleric was close to the mark. I, too, see really just two parts to the one great theme of salvation: Christ in you . . . and you in Christ. The apostle Paul sets them forth as follows:

Christ in you: "I have been crucified with Christ; it is no longer I who live, but *Christ lives in me*; and the life which I now live in the flesh I live by faith in the Son of God, who loved me and gave Himself for me" (Galatians 2:20, NKJV).

You in Christ: "But of Him [God the Father] *you are in Christ Jesus*" (1 Corinthians 1:30, NKJV).

Paul develops these twin themes in far greater detail in his epistles, but these two verses serve to summarize them.

"Christ in you" is what we often call *sanctification*—the process by which Jesus lives in us through His Spirit to bring, in real time, obedience and a character like His.

"You in Christ" is what we often call *justification*—the once-for-all act of Jesus in removing sin's penalty from us. We were forgiven at the cross. Our salvation was completed there with no effort from us. We can't add to it. We can only accept it.

"Christ in you" has to do with *power*—power to overcome, to obey, to resist temptation, to live in the Spirit rather than the "flesh." It is the fruit of salvation.

"You in Christ" has to do with *pardon*—pardon not only for our sins (plural) but for our basic inborn sin (singular) of rebellion. It is the root of salvation.

Paul, of course, is not the only Bible writer to address salvation—they all did. Some through stories. Some through symbols. Some through "theology." Some through recounting the life, teachings, death, and resurrection of Jesus.

Let's not get so lost examining individual trees that we lose track of the forest. Let's not cloud the clarity of salvation with high-sounding terminology or intellectual abstractions. Let's keep a balance between the objective facts of salvation and the subjective experience of it.

In the end, it has to be simple. Let's not pull the lifeline of salvation away from a drowning world by making tragically complicated what God made so clear and simple.

THE BLIND MEN AND THE ELEPHANT

For a whole lot of years I've enjoyed what American poet John Godfrey Saxe (1816–1887) wrote about an old fable from the country of India. He called it "The Blind Men and the Elephant."

In my book, nothing offers a better caution against becoming too opinionated, too dogmatic, too utterly certain of one's own inerrant rightness. And that can be true of organizations—even churches—as well as of people:

It was six men of Indostan
To learning much inclined,
Who went to see the Elephant
(Though all of them were blind),
That each by observation
Might satisfy his mind.

The First approached the Elephant,
And happening to fall
Against his broad and sturdy side,
At once began to bawl:
"God bless me! but the Elephant
Is very like a wall!"

The Second, feeling of the tusk,
Cried, "Ho! What have we here
So very round and smooth and sharp?
To me 'tis mighty clear
This wonder of an Elephant
Is very like a spear!"

The Third approached the animal,
And happening to take
The squirming trunk within his hands,
Thus boldly up and spake:
"I see," quoth he, "the Elephant
Is very like a snake!"

The Fourth reached out his eager hand,
And felt about the knee.
"What most this wondrous beast is like
Is mighty plain," quoth he,
"'Tis clear enough the Elephant
Is very like a tree!"

The Fifth, who chanced to touch the ear,
Said: "E'en the blindest man
Can tell what this resembles most;
Deny the fact who can,
This marvel of an Elephant
Is very like a fan!"

The Sixth no sooner had begun
About the beast to grope,
Than, seizing on the swinging tail
That fell within his scope,
"I see," quoth he, "the Elephant
Is very like a rope!"

And so these men of Indostan
Disputed loud and long,
Each in his own opinion
Exceeding stiff and strong,
Though each was partly in the right,
And all were in the wrong!

So oft, in theologic wars,
The disputants, I ween,
Rail on in utter ignorance
Of what each other mean,
And prate about an Elephant
Not one of them has seen!

Each partly in the right. Yet all—wrong. So . . . pastors, theologians, church members, editors, bloggers—all of us—we do well to dial down the absolute certainty that how *we* see truth is *the* right way.

We do well to retain a healthy quantity of humility, knowing that our eyes are too blinded to see the wholeness of truth. So there's likely a lot more to this elephant that God still has to show us than what we've already "seen."

VI. RANDOM THOUGHTS
From my Mental Hard Drive

NEVER, NEVER, NEVER, NEVER . . .

Ever felt like just quitting? cashing it in? throwing in the towel? flying the white flag? flat giving up?

• **Abraham Lincoln** was defeated in his first try for the state legislature, again defeated in his first attempt to be nominated for congress, routed in his application to be commissioner of the General Land Office, crushed in the senatorial election of 1854, failed in his efforts for the vice presidency in 1856, and defeated in the senatorial election of 1858. About that time he wrote in a letter to a friend, "I am now the most miserable man living. If what I feel were equally distributed to the whole human family, there would not be one cheerful face on earth."

• **Winston Churchill** flunked sixth grade. He subsequently lost every election for public office until he finally became prime minister when 62. He later wrote, "Never give in, never give in, never, never, never, never—in nothing, great or small, large or petty—never give in except to convictions of honor and good sense" (October 29, 1941, Harrow School).

• **Thomas Edison** was "too stupid to learn anything" (according to at least one of his teachers) and was fired from his first two jobs for being "nonproductive." As an inventor, Edison made 1,000 unsuccessful attempts at inventing the lightbulb. When a reporter asked, "How did it feel to fail 1,000 times?" Edison replied, "I didn't fail 1,000 times. The lightbulb was an invention with 1,000 steps."

• **Albert Einstein** was 4 years old before he learned how to talk, and until he turned 7 was illiterate. His mother and father decided that he was not normal, and a teacher labeled him "mentally slow, unsociable, and adrift forever in foolish dreams." At one point he found himself expelled from school. Later he failed to enter the Zurich Polytechnic School. He did eventually learn to speak and read. Even to do a little math.

• **Vince Lombardi**, an authority observed, "possesses minimal football knowledge and lacks motivation." Lombardi would later write, "It's not whether you get knocked down; it's whether you get back up."

• **Tom Landry, Chuck Noll, Bill Walsh,** and **Jimmy Johnson** were responsible for 11 of the 23 Super Bowl victories between 1972 and 1994. But they didn't always have success as coaches. During their first profootball coaching seasons they together won fewer than five games.

• **Walt Disney**, according to one newspaper editor, "lacked imagination and had no good ideas." Prior to constructing Disneyland, he had to declare bankruptcy. When he first proposed building Disneyland, the city of Anaheim rejected his plan because it would only attract riffraff.

• **Charles Schulz** of *Peanuts* fame failed to get a single cartoon printed in his high school yearbook. And Walt Disney wouldn't hire him.

• When **Jerry Seinfeld** walked onstage for the first time at a comedy club, he panicked and even forgot how to speak. He managed to muddle through about 90 seconds of comedic material, but was booed off the stage. However, on the following night vigorous clapping capped his performance.

• After **Harrison Ford's** first performance, the studio vice president summoned him and said, "Sit down, kid. I want to tell you a story. The first time Tony Curtis was ever in a movie he delivered a bag of groceries. We took one look at him and knew he was a movie star." Ford replied, "I thought you were supposed to think that he was a grocery delivery boy." The vice president dismissed Ford with "You ain't got it, kid, you ain't got it . . . now get out of here."

• **Enrico Caruso's** voice teacher said he could not sing, and his mother and father thought he should go into engineering.

• Decca Records refused to contract with the **Beatles** and complained: "We don't like their sound. Groups of guitars are on their way out." Columbia Records likewise denied giving them a contract.

• The administrator of the Grand Ole Opry, Jimmy Denny, dismissed **Elvis Presley** after one performance, informing Presley, "You ain't goin' nowhere, son. You ought to go back to drivin' a truck."

• Eighteen different publishers turned down **Richard Bach's** story about a "soaring eagle." Macmillan finally published *Jonathan Livingston Seagull* in 1970, and by five years later it had sold more than 9 million copies. (Total sales to date: 40 million.)

• Finally, **Jesus** never gave up on the rebellious, doomed human race. He has never given up on you—and He never will. So never give up on your hopes and dreams of what you can do or become. Never give up on yourself or on anybody else!

WHATEVER HAPPENED TO COMMON SENSE?

For a second there, I almost rubbed my eyes. "Natural Tastes Better," promised the full-page ad. Against a background of sun rays sat a box . . . of cigarettes. Natural American Spirit cigs, to be specific—a brand I hadn't heard of before. But the real attention-grabber was the subheading: "100 Percent Additive-Free Natural Tobacco."

Ah, yes—cigarettes as part of your personal health program! No point in risking any of those lethal, unnatural additives as you're pumping your lungs full of your normal dose of tar and nicotine.

So I sez to myself, I sez: "How brain-damaged do these tobacco marketers think we are? Do they really think they can sell cancer sticks as somehow more healthful because now they're 'natural'? Whatever happened to common sense?"

And that's where my thoughts headed next—to the apparent scarcity of common sense. Do the wizards who make TV commercials really think we'll put our brains on pause so they can crank up the volume, push all our knee-jerk impulsive buttons, and hide their warnings in print so fine a microscope can't see it?

Apparently they do. And apparently we do.

It's not just in commerce that too many of us abandon common sense. It happens in the wild overreactions of the stock market, in the fickle voter responses that cause constantly switching allegiances, in the spiritual choices people make.

Yes. Even in religion—even in church. Some of the most nonsensical, harebrained, fruity ideas on earth show up in the arena of religion. Preachers who say God sends hurricanes to punish wrong votes on abortion. Members who accuse everybody else of heresy or apostasy if other people don't see things exactly as they do. Parents who let their kids die because their religious belief doesn't include doctors and hospitals.

God gave each of us a good brain. We come with common sense built in. But God also gave us the power of choice. That means that our brains have an on-off switch.

When we move our common sense—our reason—to the off position, anything goes. We end up believing that it's a sin to eat pork but OK to cannibalize the reputation of fellow church members. We end up thinking "natural" cigarettes are really a great leap forward in good health!

WHY PEACE GETS A BUM RAP

Peace gets a bad rap. War is macho: guns and explosions, blood and guts, winning and losing. And where war isn't available, we'll manufacture vegetarian versions of it: football (replete with war metaphors), video games, violent movies, boxing, and wrestling.

But peace? Peace is for sissies and wusses. It's wimpy and boring and lacks enough testosterone. Perhaps there's a reason women are often at the forefront of anti-war movements. And along with women are the weak-kneed Christians. Their leader is even called the Prince of Peace. Then again, maybe women and Christians are onto something.

Perhaps we ought to remember that conflict is an aberration, an intruder. Before Lucifer, it never existed. And once Lucifer goes, conflict goes with him. He is the one who tried to deify self—the ultimate goal of which is "I'm first, and if necessary to defend that position, I'll destroy you." Self readily resorts to force to get what it wants. But again, before Lucifer, force never existed.

Those of us infected with the virus of selfishness that Lucifer let loose have warped perceptions of reality. It's as if our wiring is in backward so that we love (or are at least drawn to) conflict and hate (or are at least bored by) peace—rather than the other way around, as God created us. So couples and churches and political parties and nations constantly stir the pot, thriving on the drama of self. Even just the idea of me-first brings an adrenaline rush—as Eve found while listening to the serpent's sales pitch.

Conflict on earth is now so systemic that peace seems the aberration. Conflict is a basic and endemic reality of daily life.

- It could be two small schoolboys duking it out on the playground.
- Maybe it's a husband and wife arguing—trading harsh, bitter words.
- It could be two prizefighters in a ring, intent on punching each other's lights out.
- It could be the shouting of TV "talking heads" generating more heat than light about politics.
- It could be two nations, posturing and threatening—or actively engaged in combat.
- It is even likely that often you're aware of a fight taking place right inside you—a fight between your good side and your not-so-good side.

But God is a God of peace, not conflict. He created a world of total and perfect peace—of complete harmony between people. Even the animals were at peace with each other. An utter lack of conflict is God's ideal—though most assuredly, when those He created and loved were threatened, He proved demonstrably ready to defend them even to the death. Peaceful does not equate with passive. The great controversy between good and evil does have two sides—but the conflict is not God's original or ultimate will. Fortunately, the Bible makes clear that a time is coming soon when again, this earth will be a place of absolute peace.

In that new earth, will we have challenges? Of course. Will we have ways of testing ourselves? Yes, but not against each other.

Here in this life, conflict seems strong and peace seems weak. That is only because Satan has successfully sold that bill of goods. The truth is, in our current sinful environment, it takes enormous strength to seek peace. To opt for conflict only requires the easy choice of not resisting our worst impulses.

Yet another way that God sees things differently from His end of the telescope—than we do through our end here on earth.

ON DRIVING STRAIGHT INTO A NEW-AGE FOGBANK

You know what? I happen to really, really enjoy New Age music. It is peaceful and soothing, and when it's there in the background, it seems to stimulate or enhance creativity.

But it's partly in connection with that word *creativity* that I have to part ways with New Age philosophy. Truth is, I wish New Age music had some other name, because it's too beautiful to be linked to New Age teaching, which I couldn't ever buy into even if they threatened me with 17 varieties of torture.

Notice this excerpt from a post I found today on one of the Internet's most-read blogs:

"In fact, it is the very nature of the Self to create. You are imbued with infinite creative potential. . . . Creativity is the essence of divinity. As you awaken to your true divine nature, you can access the vast creative power inherent in the heart of your being."

Now, see, I can agree that God, as the Creator, gave to each of us the gift of creativity. I also believe that through His Spirit, God wants to dwell in us—in some mysterious way—to actually indwell our minds and change us from the inside out.

Where I part ways with the New Agers is that they teach we are creative because we are *inherently divine*—and need only to discover our natural, inborn divinity in order to accomplish a lot of divine things.

Often as I peruse a bit of New Age information, I ask myself why—if this philosophy is presumably so divine and heavenly—it comes across as such *utter, nonsensical gobbledygook!*

Read this from the same blog post—and if you understand it, please send me the translation!

"Creation is not about attracting objects to you, it's about entering the Divine Mind which holds all things simultaneously in indistinguishable unity. Here you are nondifferent from that which you desire to create. Thought and form are inseparable, an idea and its physical expression are indivisible. By collapsing subject and object, you become infinite. Now, the true yogic secret is revealed: if you drop a single thought into the thought-free Divine Mind, it will have atomic power to manifest."

SAY *WHAT?*

Can it perhaps be that when human beings begin to fancy themselves as being inherently divine, rather than becoming more creative and precise, they become hopelessly confused and confusing? Can it perhaps be that in attempting to sound sophisticated and hyperintellectual, they instead come across more like kindergarten children creating a hodgepodge of words out of letter blocks?

I still enjoy New Age music—probably always will. But deliver me from its pretentious, esoteric philosophy!

THE PHILOSOPHER FORREST GUMP

In the movie based on the above character, Forrest Gump is given to sharing his guiding life philosophy, learned from his "mama." Hence, "*My mama always said, 'Life was like a box of chocolates.'*"

Another of his principles surfaced when people unkindly questioned his intelligence: "*My mama always said, 'Stupid is as stupid does.'*"

In other words, "Judge people by what they do, not by how they appear."

Fair enough, Forrest.

But what are we to make of the growing tsunami of "stupid doing" sweeping the cultural landscape? What can we say of the elevation of "dumbness" to a place of pride and status? Should it be of concern that stupidity passes for high entertainment in the media? Do we have anything to say about the juvenile, scatological, foul-mouthed, and sophomoric crudity; the sniggering, moronic, and utter brainless "humor" that—unless we retreat from civilization—floods our senses daily? And for that matter, can we any longer even legitimately use the word *civilization* with any credibility?

Where does one even start in citing examples? Beavis and Butthead. The Simpsons. Miss Teen South Carolina struggling to express a single coherent sentence. Rap music with its all-too-often utterly inane, gutter-level, violent lyrics. Howard Stern and his grade-school-level obsession with all things crude and imbecilic. MTV's *Jackass*. Jay Leno's "Jaywalking," in which people are clueless as to when the War of 1812 took place.

For that matter, the movie *Clueless* of a few years back. Or *Dumb and Dumber*. Young actors who specialize in starring in a vacuous, obscene, and profanity-laced brand of "comedy" that bears no resemblance to the humor of such earlier-generation comedians as Lucille Ball, Dick Van Dyke, Carol Burnett, Don Knotts, and many others.

The crowd of vapid, directionless "party girls" (you know their names) famous and envied for contributing absolutely nothing of any lasting value to the world in which they live.

We live in a society in which real intelligence, "being smart," knowing things, is considered by the young as a stigma. A high GPA is for eggheads and losers. Acceptance comes through winning at how much booze you can hold as it's poured through a funnel.

We live in a society in which far too many prize the hedonistic, self-indulgent, and peer-pressure-driven pursuit of instant sensory gratification over cultivation of thought, maturation, and personal development.

It's embarrassing to realize that my dad fought in World War II to provide the freedom for today's generation to prize stupidity and cluelessness. It's embarrassing that studies show a steady decline in IQs in each younger generation. It's embarrassing for me as an editor to receive manuscripts from college-educated writers who struggle to express themselves on a third-grade level.

Many books survey this bleak landscape, among them *The Dumbest Generation,* by Emory University professor Mark Bauerlein, and *The Age of American Unreason,* by Susan Jacoby.

Religion, my frame of reference in this book, has contributed its own share to the ascending anti-intellectualism—consider the "know nothing" authoritarianism and chauvinistic misogyny seen in secretive cults; the heavy-handed discouragement of open questioning and investigation of truth in many churches; or the machoistic love of guns and war and strutting toughness by those whose Leader is presumably the Prince of Peace.

Yes, I know that the Bible says that as we race to the final act in history's sad drama, we'll see a "time of trouble such as never was." All the "straws in the wind" are flying in that direction: global warming, increasing religiopolitical devotion to coercive legislation of morality and behavior while steadily stripping away personal freedoms, an economy teetering on the raw edge of sudden collapse, a world running out of resources, the rich getting richer and the poor even poorer, and the deification of dumbness.

The world we once knew, friends and neighbors, is no more and never will be again. It's time to brace ourselves for the unraveling of social order, the disintegration of a tired and misery-racked world, even as it morphs into a reality beyond anything George Orwell's *1984* or Ellen White's *Great Controversy* could fully detail.

Convinced of this, I choose to give the cult of dumbness a wide berth. I'm dismayed that so many accept—even take a baseless pride in—ignorance and intellectual laziness as a perfectly fine way to live. I've seen and heard enough superficiality and mindless dreck to last me several lifetimes.

Death and depression and disease and divorce and discouragement and . . . dumbness. Anything in common here? A clue? Yet another word beginning with "d" . . . the name of the CEO of everything demonic and diabolical.

But please hold strong to your hope and courage. It may get worse before it gets better. But when it gets better, the positive will utterly eradicate the negative.

Check the final two verses of Revelation 22 now and then for the needed reminder of how the story ends.

DID GOD RESIGN?

Listening to cable news, I heard one of the lofty talking heads speaking during the 2008 presidential race as he advanced his towering wisdom that the candidates were running for "the most important job in the universe."

Uh . . . say what? Run that by me again.

Yes, I know that the media yakkers really do seem to think that the headquarters of the universe is in Washington, D.C., if not at 1600 Pennsylvania Avenue. But last I heard, "the most important job in the universe" was already filled—and it's not an elected position. And I haven't heard that God has resigned.

In fact, if you agree with me that besides the Father, Son, and Holy Spirit, the jobs of about a gazillion angels are also more important than the president of one country on a tiny polluted planet in a remote outpost solar system far from heaven—well, if you agree with that, then the candidates are running for, at best, "the one-gazillion-and-fourth most important job in the universe."

Human ego. Sometimes it's so disconnected from reality that you don't know whether to laugh or mourn.

THE VIEW FROM SIX MILES UP

On those occasions that I'm tooling along at 500 miles per hour up there at 30,000 feet in my "spacious" coach seat in a metal tube, I tend to get reflective about what I see down below.

Passing over great American cities (on one recent flight I could see Phoenix, St. Louis, Las Vegas, Albuquerque, Louisville, and Tulsa, among others), I'm always impressed by the sheer number of residences down there. Some suburban areas seem carpeted wall-to-wall with cookie-cutter homes wearing their Spanish-tile roofs, each house with a turquoise pool out back. Inner-city dwellings of early-twentieth-century vintage are sans pools, but these older homes are not clones of each other.

More rural areas have large ranch homes on green acreage, and triple-wide mobile home parks sprawl across some desert retirement communities.

I've also flown over cities such as Mexico City, where the sea of dwellings seems to stretch horizon to horizon.

Thousands of homes. Tens of thousands. In millions of cities and towns around this globe. And in each of them, people live out their daily lives. Each home, could its walls talk, would tell a story of its current and former dwellers.

Those stories would chronicle joy and pain, laughter and despair, birthdays and anniversaries, violence and abuse, newborns and those in their final days of life. And as I soar over them all, I'm oblivious to all the human drama six miles beneath me. Couples embracing. Robberies in progress. Hospital patients fighting back searing pain. Business deals a-making. Kids playing. Teenagers hanging out. Students taking notes. Workers working and bosses bossing. The homeless. The starving. Couples being wed. Junkies shooting up. Athletes pushing the limits. The first breath and cry. The last breath and sigh. The loving and hating and cheating and achieving. The giving and the giving up. The smiles, the tears, the hopes, the fears.

And unlike me from my aeronautic perch, God sees it all. He knows it all. He knows every resident in all those countless homes and offices and schools—and those who have no homes—by name. He loves each as if that man, woman, child, or infant were the only one alive in this universe. He gave His life for every one of them.

If I truly believed that God's perspective—far more inclusive than mine, since He sees the entire world—made it possible for Him to see all and know all, but in disengaged detachment, I'd turn my back on Him and never look back. For how could He see not just the happinesses but the sorrows and miseries, yet remain unmoved?

But I happen to believe that God does care. He knows every burden and feels every discouragement and broken heart.

For reasons I may not fully learn till we're all on the other side, God doesn't just unfailingly step in and deliver, intervene, and set right. But it means everything to me that He not only sees but also cares and is *with* me in my trials—that He truly is "God *with* us."

"Please return your seat backs and tray tables to their full upright and locked position."

Another reverie interrupted. But I need these occasional chances to see things just a little more from God's point of view.

WHY iDON'T NEED AN iPHONE

On one internet news site I check frequently, I ran across an item about a mansion for sale in Beverly Hills for $165 million—to that moment, the highest price ever commanded for a private residence in the U.S.

The place originally belonged to newspaper baron William Randolph Hearst (same chap who built the impossibly opulent Hearst Castle on the California coast).

The BevHills residence has 29 bedrooms (is this a house or a hotel?), three swimming pools, a movie theater, a disco, and an undisclosed number of bathrooms. The property has five other residences and tennis courts here and there on its 6.5 acres.

With half of the world's 6.6 billion people living on less than $2 a day (millions of them starving to death) this kind of "conspicuous consumption"—this incredible excess—seems obscene in the extreme.

Yet the urge for "more" is in all of us, and on that fault, I don't get a free pass over anyone else. I'm fairly sure I could enjoy a Caddy Escalade big enough for its own zip code (at least till the first stop at the gas pump), instead of my current aging wheels. But I don't *need* it. And though I don't *need* 29 bedrooms, I'd like to build my dream home overlooking the Oregon coast or on a forested mountainside.

Like a lot of males, I also have the gene that enjoys high-tech stuff: computers, cell phones, digital cameras—that sort of thing. I suppose even a wall-to-wall plasma TV with a surround-sound system to wake the dead could hold its charms. And the latest iPhone that's a Swiss army knife of techno-awesomeness? That could keep me fiddling for hours while my work burned.

My "wanter" is just as alive and well as anyone else's, I'm quite sure. But when I look at this whole area of possessions—of "stuff"—my best reason tells me that I certainly don't *need* and can't justify everything I might want.

If you have a new iPhone and truly need it, blessings on you—and you'll get no judging from me about it. But as much as it might be great to have a gizmo that combines a cell phone and camera with wireless Internet and a personal organizer and makes breakfast every morning, I know that I personally can't yet justify and don't *need* an iPhone. I already have a phone that does more things than I'll ever need or have time to figure out.

There's still something to be said for the old-fashioned virtue of frugality. And there's plenty also that's good about learning to be content with what one already has rather than constantly chasing the endless "more."

Our Christianity should also inform this discussion. For one thing, the essence of selfishness is to hoard to oneself—to get, to have, to acquire. The essence of love, on the other hand, is to give.

For another, though we need not feel guilty about having—or striving for—a comfortable level of material security in this life, the realization that half the world's people live in starvation and abject poverty should temper our attitudes and decisions about tangible possessions.

This topic deserves a full book—not just a few paragraphs. But as I preach to myself occasionally, I don't mind if you listen in.

YOUR TOP 10 GOALS

You can find a Web site on any conceivable topic these days. One that draws a lot of traffic is 43 Things—a goal-sharing site.

Based on the expressed goals of their visitors, here's their list (as of the day of this post) of the all-time top personal goals. I'll list here only the top 10 of their current top 100:

1. Lose weight.
2. Stop procrastinating.
3. Fall in love.
4. Write a book.
5. Be happy.
6. Get a tattoo.
7. Drink more water.
8. Go on a road trip with no predetermined destination.
9. Get married.
10. Travel the world.

Now, I'm not going to overly criticize this list. In fact, I'd say at least five of these top goals are on my own personal list—and some of the others, I've already accomplished.

I could live another 500 years, though, and *never* want to do number 6. How on earth can there really be that many people for whom getting a tattoo is one of their top 10 goals in life?

Some observations on the 43 Things list:

• I can only applaud the whole idea of setting and working toward personal goals. If you aim at nothing, you will most certainly hit it. As that great philosopher Yogi Berra said: "If you don't know where you are going, you'll end up someplace else."

• And as perhaps a more credible philosopher—the poet Robert Browning—said: "Ah, but a man's reach should exceed his grasp, or what's a heaven for?" Like many others, I set and track goals in all major areas of my life: mental, physical, spiritual, financial, relational, vocational, and recreational.

• In general, the above list seems heavily "me"-oriented. Where's something about "be a better parent," "be more giving to my spouse," or "find ways to help those in need"?

• The list on this Web site reflects not a single goal that includes a spiritual or Christian element. Even in reading not just the top 10 but the top 100 goals listed on the site, I see not one about getting to know God better, living out the golden rule, or doing all the good I possibly can.

Question for reflection: Whether you're a top 10 or top 43 goal person, what are your goals? And what do your personal goals say about you, your life, your priorities, the people around you, and your view of God and eternity?

VII. SNAPSHOTS OF
Something Called "Church"

CHRISTIANITY'S IMAGE:
TIME FOR AN EXTREME MAKEOVER

Christianity has developed a severe image problem. Many Christians—especially those of the most conservative variety—see the church as besieged by a wave of secularism. They have settled into a militant and somewhat paranoiac stance against what they are convinced is a godless culture out to at least ridicule—if not persecute—them and their beliefs.

And in that militancy, many Christians—including and perhaps especially high-profile Christian leaders—have taken to lashing out at the prevailing secular culture. They call down God's judgments on all who do not share their pro-God, pro-life, pro-family values.

Now, let's assume that most of these values are good and truly biblical (though as sometimes defined, some could be questioned on that count). If so, how far has it gotten the church to condemn and judge the sinners around it? As Dr. Phil asks: "How is that working for you?"

Apparently, not very well. Recent research among young people 16 through 29 by the Barna Group, a California-based research center, shows that today's younger generation is giving the church and Christianity mostly a failing grade.

The Barna Group's president, David Kinnaman, reported on that research in a book entitled *unChristian: What a New Generation Really Thinks About Christianity.*

By large percentages, young people said that the Christian community is judgmental, hypocritical, and anti-gay.

The majority of the survey participants were non-Christians. Of those, 85 percent said Christianity is hypocritical; 87 percent said it is judgmental; and 91 percent said it is anti-gay.

The young Christians who were surveyed had, perhaps not surprisingly, a somewhat better view of themselves: 47 percent said Christianity is hypocritical, 52 percent that it is judgmental, and 80 percent that it is anti-gay.

The research discovered that even among the Christians, many no longer want to call themselves by that name because of the baggage that comes with that label. Some now call themselves "followers of Jesus" or "apprentices of Christ." Even Kinnaman, himself only 33, now describes himself as "a committed Christ follower."

"Our goal wasn't simply to say here's all the problems, but to hopefully point a way forward," Kinnaman said.

"When Jesus pursued people," he added, "He was much more critical of pride and much more critical of spiritual arrogance than He was of people who were sinful. And today's Christians, if you spend enough time looking at their attitudes and actions, really are not like Jesus when it comes to that."

Megachurch pastor Rick Warren of Saddleback Church in Lake Forest, California (and best-selling author of *The Purpose Driven Life),* in commenting on Kinnaman's research, said he wishes the church could become "known more by what it is for than what it is against. For some time now, the hands and feet of the body of Christ have been amputated, and we've been pretty much reduced to a big mouth. We talk more than we do."

And apparently what Christians are saying is not winning the world to Christ but driving them away from Him. It's the old honey-works-better-than-vinegar principle. You get further attracting people—whether it's the godless secularists around us or a potential spouse—by leaving out the judging and condemning.

An Adventist writer once said this:

"The people of the world are worshiping false gods. They are to be turned from their false worship, not by hearing denunciations of their idols, but by beholding something better. God's goodness is to be made known" (*Christ's Object Lessons,* p. 299).

• Perhaps we should ask whether it's our job to condemn sinners and their sins, or whether it's the work of the Holy Spirit instead to do that convicting.

• Perhaps we might get further in dealing with even such a specific departure from God's perfect will as homosexuality by bringing on the love rather than the condemnation.

• Perhaps we might remember that only those without sin are qualified to throw stones.

• Perhaps we might remember, too, that our mission is to lift up Jesus, not declare war on sinners and call down upon them His divine judgments.

• Perhaps Rick Warren is spot-on accurate: It's time we became known for what we are *for*—not what we're *against.*

As Christians, we can become defensive and self-justifying in the face of research such as that done by the Barna Group. We can rationalize our status quo and find ways to prove non-Christians wrong. But the fact remains that as today's young people see the church, it's turning them away—and it does not represent very well its namesake Leader.

And the solution—if we don't like what we see in the mirror that's been held up to us—is not to trash the mirror but to ask God for an extreme makeover.

If we must be at war with the sinful pagans around us, then let's attack them with overwhelming force, with the most potent of all weapons: the limitless power of God's accepting, approving, forgiving, restoring, and life-changing love.

MYSPACE, FACEBOOK, AND YOUTUBE: THE POWER OF SOCIAL NETWORKING

In my lifetime I've seen huge changes. As a kid I remember the dealership in my hometown selling new Chevys for $1,795. As a young man, I paid 17.9 cents for a gallon of gas. In college I laboriously typed my term papers using an old Smith-Corona typewriter, carbon paper, and Wite-Out correction fluid (some of these terms will be total mysteries to current and younger generations).

But the pace of change has accelerated exponentially. Computers showed up as a consumer item in the 1980s, rendering typewriters obsolete. A decade or so later the Internet arrived. And yet another decade brought the truly amazing current phenomenon of digital and Internet social networking.

From earlier avenues of social communication such as chat rooms and e-mail, networking today has evolved into an amazing variety of channels: blogs, wikis, instant messaging, text messaging, file-sharing sites (YouTube, Flickr, Napster and then Kazaa and others), and now such lively social networks as MySpace, Facebook, Xanga, Bebo, Classmates.com, Orkut, Friendster, and others.

As a Christian, I can never really see my world without looking at it through Christian lenses. And as I've witnessed the runaway success of these vehicles of social networking, I've wondered about their implications for people of faith. In no particular order, some thoughts:

• If people can become so interconnected socially through these various channels (this very blog is an example of one person communicating and inviting communication in return), what are the possibilities for spiritual networking? Of course, that's ostensibly one purpose of the church. Christians call it fellowship. I wonder if church leaders and Christians in general have given much thought to the demonstrated success of Internet social networking—if they've brainstormed the potential this implies for social-spiritual networking? To some degree, of course, this is already happening. But does the phenomenal success of current social networking have anything to suggest to Christians for achieving greater fellowship and unity than ever before?

• What does the stunning growth of social networking say to Christians in terms of outreach? in terms of winning others to the God we love? Clearly, this global spiderweb of communication is meeting very real human needs. What are those? Are there opportunities here for sharing? for linking people not just with each other but with Jesus?

• Are we quite certain as Christians that the church is adapting to societal and cultural changes quickly enough? While the good news of the gospel is unchanging, does it serve us well if we are slow to change our methods? What may have worked well in the 1940s, 1960s, 1980s, or even at the turn of the millennium may not be as effective in 2010. Is the Christian church keeping pace with the times—taking advantage of promising new opportunities made possible in this digital age?

• Much of the content of the current wave of social networking is quite superficial . . . little more than idle chatter and public diary writing. Some of it is more thoughtful, of course—blogs in particular seem to be a more reflective form of sharing. But can we find ways to present the Christian message through these new electronic avenues in ways that will captivate and attract people to something higher than trivial, largely self-focused concerns?

I'm probably a little old for a MySpace page, though I do find some video gems on YouTube, and play Last.fm music while I'm pounding the keyboard—and have recently enjoyed venturing forth into blogging. But as I see the explosion of communication and connecting taking place through cell phones and computers—text, voice, images, video, and music—I can only wonder what the possibilities are for improved spiritual fellowship and outreach.

SUNDAY LAWS IN AMERICA

My work involves, among other tasks, editing and preparing for publication materials for a wide variety of clients. A while back I worked on a book setting forth the history of so-called Sunday blue laws.

The very first such law was enacted in the colony of Virginia in 1610, and read as follows:

"Every man and woman shall repair in the morning to the divine service and sermons preached upon the Sabbath day, and in the afternoon to divine service, and catechizing, upon pain for the first fault to lose their provision and the allowance for the whole week following; for the second, to lose the said allowance and also be whipt; and for the third to suffer death."

Get that? Attend services both morning and afternoon—or face the early-American version of "three strikes and you're out." Strike one: lose your food allowance for a week. Strike two: lose your food allowance for a week and be whipped. Strike three: kiss your life goodbye. And this was not some totalitarian country—some atheistic dictatorship such as China or North Korea or Cuba. Nor was it some theocratic regime such as Iran. It was colonial America.

Other colonies besides Virginia had their own Sunday laws, requiring attendance at services and forbidding everything from working to sports and recreation to swearing and "tippling" at the taverns. Punishments included fines of money and up to 200 pounds of tobacco, being locked in the public stocks, jailtime, and again, in "grievous" cases, death.

Captain Kemble of Boston, Massachusetts, was in 1656 locked in the public stocks for two hours for kissing his wife on the Sabbath (Sunday) after spending three years at sea. The charge? "Unseemly behavior."

Even newly elected president George Washington was not exempt from punishment under Sabbath laws in 1789. As he traveled from Connecticut to a town in New York to attend worship service one Sunday, Washington was detained by a tithingman for violating Connecticut's law forbidding unnecessary travel on Sunday. Washington was permitted to continue on his journey only after he promised to go no farther than his destination town.

While this early religious legislation in America may sound inflexible and harsh, it's the natural and inevitable result of removing the wall of separation between church and state—between religion and government. It's the sure end when some attempt to force the consciences and moral behaviors of others.

And some of us believe that as that wall of separation continues to crumble in the United States, the likelihood is great, should that effort fully succeed, of an America in which once again penalties could be exacted by the state for religious violations—penalties up to and including death.

The intolerant militancy of America's extreme Religious Right should give anyone who prizes true religious freedom pause. Many leaders and jurists of the Religious Right either deny the religious-freedom protections intended by the first amendment or hope to change or abolish that amendment.

As government, in the name of national security, strips away certain rights of its citizens and intrudes into their privacy and as the religiopolitical right becomes increasingly aggressive in attempting to legislate personal morality and behavior, the likelihood also increases that at some point, mandatory church attendance—and on a day incompatible with the beliefs of many—could certainly come up for a congressional vote.

America once imposed the death penalty for those in violation of compulsory Sunday church attendance. All signs point to the strong possibility that history could be repeated, even here in the land of the "so-far" free.

Even were I a Sundaykeeping Christian, I'd find this use of state legislation to enforce religious observance troubling or even appalling. As a Saturday Sabbathkeeping Christian, my concern and watchfulness is understandably even greater.

CHANGING CHURCHES, AND A CHANGING CHURCH

If there's one word popular during political campaigns, it's likely to be *change*. But it's not just in politics that, as Bob Dylan once sang, "the times, they are a-changin'."

A report from the Pew Forum on Religion and Public Life underscores the great degree of change taking place in Christian churches across the United States. Among its highlights:

• Forty-four percent of American adults have changed religious affiliation since childhood. That includes those raised outside a religious tradition who later joined a particular faith and the 28 percent of people who either left their childhood faith and now don't belong to any religious group or who have switched from one denomination to another.

• Sixteen percent of Americans don't identify with any religion, including 25 percent of those ages 18 to 29. This percentage is nonetheless far lower than in other industrialized countries, experts say, meaning that the United States remains by comparison a strongly religious country.

• Twenty-four percent of the population is Roman Catholic, a percentage that hasn't changed in recent decades. Almost one third of those reared as Catholics have left the faith, but immigration—especially from Latin America—has kept the denomination's numbers steady.

• Thirty-seven percent of married people are married outside their faith.

THREE PEAS IN A POD

In a post on his blog Faith in Context entitled "Christians As Pop Culture Wannabes," Monte Sahlin added his thoughts to those of writer Loren Seibold, on the topic of how we Christians should relate to the culture—the "world"—around us.

Monte describes two typical Christian responses:

"Unfortunately, most Christian responses to the current cultural context fall into two categories: (1) putting 'head in sand,' ignoring contemporary culture or reacting against it in such sweeping tones as to disconnect from society and live in a Christian bubble, or (2) behave like 'wannabes.'"

But Monte goes on to propose a third alternative, which he calls "culturally creative engagement"—finding ways to impact the society around us positively.

This discussion reminded me of an illustration I heard a long time back, which I included in a chapter as I was writing—a few years ago—the centennial history for Loma Linda University Adventist Health Sciences Center, entitled *Railway to the Moon:*

Three peas lived happily in a pod. Came the day, however, when the pod opened slightly to reveal the rich brown soil below. One pea shrank back in alarm. "The soil is dirty," said the first pea. "We're safe here in our pod. We're green—and should stay as far away from the brown soil as possible."

The second pea had other ideas. Feeling restricted by the pod and odd being green while surrounded by so much brown, it quickly wriggled free of the pod and rolled around in the soil to get as brown as possible—as quickly as possible.

The third pea surveyed the soil and said, "You know, we're all green. The soil is brown. Green is just the color the soil needs to see more of." And with that, the third pea rolled onto the soil and shared its "green-ness" with the brown earth.

Christians sometimes struggle in relating to the world around them. Some separate themselves as far as possible from "the world" so it can't soil them. Others don't like to be so different—as different as green is from brown—and they plunge into the world so that they won't stand out. Finally, some Christians step boldly into the world to share their true colors and make the brown world a greener place.

WHY I'VE BECOME AN ATHEIST

Yes, I've decided that "God" doesn't exist. Don't get me wrong. I'm not signing on with Bertrand Russell, who in *Why I Am Not a Christian* said he could not believe in a God who condemned people to everlasting punishment.

I'm not agreeing with Mark Twain, who wrote: "If there is a God, He is a malign thug"—or the now-departed Madalyn Murray O'Hair (*Why I Am an Atheist*)—whom I once personally interviewed at her Austin, Texas, home for a feature story.

I'm not following Ted Turner in giving up on God. When—as Ted was growing up—his younger sister died of lupus, his father said, "If that's the type of God He is, I want nothing to do with Him." Soon after, Ted's father killed himself—and shortly thereafter, Ted himself abandoned any semblance of faith.

Nor have I been persuaded by the arguments of current atheistic authors Christopher Hitchens (*God Is Not Great*), Richard Dawkins (*The God Delusion*), or Sam Harris (*The End of Faith*).

No, don't get me wrong. Despite plenty of unanswered questions, I still believe in the God of the Bible—the God who is the Creator and ruler of the universe—the God of three persons: Father, Son, and Holy Spirit.

But I categorically do not believe in the fictional god so many—even Christians—claim today to worship.

Case in point from a news report:

"A jury on Wednesday ordered an anti-gay Kansas church to pay $10.9 million in damages to relatives of a U.S. Marine after church members cheered his death at his funeral."

Marine Lance Corporal Matthew Snyder died in combat in Iraq in March of 2006. At his funeral members of the nondenominationally affiliated Westboro Baptist Church in Topeka, Kansas, interrupted the services, holding up signs reading "God Hates Fags" while loudly shouting anti-gay epithets.

Corporal Snyder's father stated that his son had not been gay. But in the space of two years the church demonstrated at more than 200 servicemen's funerals, targeting the military as a symbol of America's tolerance of gays. Not surprisingly, the church also believes that Hurricane Katrina, the September 11 attacks, and AIDS are all God's judgments for permissive American morals.

So I can't believe in the god worshipped by the Westboro Baptist Church. Why? I'm convinced he doesn't exist. I believe there IS no god who "hates fags"—or, for that matter, who loathes murderers, terrorists, adulterers, genocidal dictators, or corrupt politicians.

I also believe there is no god who calls down punishing judgments at the behest of such clergymen as Pat Robertson and the late Jerry Falwell. There is no god who condemns and hates—and monitors the planet for any sign of human weakness so that he may rain down judgments.

Yes, I still believe in the God who is love. The God who hates sin, yes . . . but loves the sinner. The God who motivates with love, not fear. The God who warns us that the natural consequence of sin—should we refuse to let Him separate us from it—is misery and, ultimately, death.

Since there is a true God, it is no mystery that Satan the enemy goads human beings into creating false ones—fictional beings of wrath, intolerance, judgment, condemnation, and impatience. Some of those gods may be called "Allah"; others, "God."

And when those who claim to be Christians or God-believers—whatever their home-church faith may be—present to the world these false gods, the world recoils from such an unpleasant deity. It hardens into doubt, resentment, hostility, cynicism, agnosticism, and atheism.

Yes, I too am an atheist when it comes to the "god" of Westboro, a god even some who claim God's name present as real. That god is NOT real. He doesn't exist. And I, for one, will never depart from that atheism.

WHEN DID "AMEN" BECOME A QUESTION?

I've been one—and the role of a pastor is not an easy one. So I'm reluctant to question those already carrying a full load. I also consciously try to stay on the positive side of the line in life, so I'm hoping the following observation will be seen as "constructive criticism."

The word *amen* is a good Bible word. It can be translated from the original languages into such English declarations as "verily," "so be it," "truly," or even the colloquial "preach it, brother!"

Some churches are filled with frequent *amens* as the Word is preached. Some are as silent as a tomb. Now, charge me perhaps with stirring up a tempest in a teapot, but I truly believe the good word *amen* should be a spontaneous, unsolicited, and heartfelt declaration—and not a preacher's question in an effort to go fishing for audience response that otherwise might not be forthcoming.

Hypothetical example: "I believe it's high time we do more than just believe," the parson states with conviction. "We need to start *doing* what we believe!" Then he quickly adds the question "Amen?" Or "Can you say amen to that?"

In other words: "Would somebody out there *please* speak up and agree?"

This trend seems especially to have taken hold in evangelistic preaching and among some who preach on TV. I recently watched a young televangelist pacing the stage like a caged lion with the caffeine jitters, imploring the "brothers and sisters" with a steady repetition of the question "Amen?" at the end of seemingly every other sentence.

But my own view of it is that if the preacher's words are powerful and true and Spirit-generated enough, the amens will become spontaneous and not uncommon, with no need to plead or beg for them.

Verily and so be it.

YAHOO, NETSCAPE, WORDPERFECT, AND CHRISTIANITY

I've been into computers practically from day one. Not in the geeky sense, but more as, first, an area of "hobby"-style interest and, later, as someone whose livelihood is computer-based.

My first computer was a Commodore VIC-20. I attended the seventh annual West Coast Computer Faire in San Francisco in 1982 and the first Seybold Computer Publishing Conference and Exposition there a couple of years later.

I progressed through a Commodore 64, then the first floppy-drive-only IBM PC, and on through several hardware changes to my present HP widescreen laptop and an HP desktop with all the bells and whistles.

But it's in the software arena that I've lived through something that has implications for every living Christian—including me.

Repeatedly I've seen a software package become dominant in its class, only to lose its perch in time to a competitor. Early on, dBase had the database field almost entirely to itself. Then it couldn't figure out how to move from DOS to the newfangled Windows operating system fast enough and was soon passed up by programs such as Paradox, FoxPro, and Access.

Even in pre-Windows days, those of us who cut our teeth on DOS used only one word processor: WordPerfect. It ruled with nearly total hegemony. Then the company was sold and resold, lost its vision, and Microsoft Word passed it up and still dominates the category.

When the Internet burst on the scene in the 1990s, it wasn't long before Netscape was the 1,000-pound gorilla of browsers. Microsoft's Internet Explorer started with a microscopic market share but persisted till it utterly replaced Netscape, which a few days ago announced the end of any support for the browser. These days we may be witnessing a repeat of this cycle, as Firefox continues to gain market share on IE.

The same has happened with Lotus 1-2-3 to Excel, or Ventura Publisher to InDesign. And in recent years we watched the same thing happen as Google sent Yahoo reeling.

Many factors figure in the decline of once-dominant companies or software packages: slowness to adapt, buyouts by companies that don't know or care how to make their purchase work, or sudden technology shifts that bring instant obsolescence.

But perhaps the most needless and deadly reason that giants fall is because of one word: *complacency.* Taking their success and customers for granted, companies get lazy. Once lean and responsive, they become hobbled in bureaucracy and process charts and paper shuffling.

Complacency: the great enemy of success. It's deadly to companies. But also to relationships, to personal accomplishment, and—here's the link to Christianity—to churches and individual Christians.

Both churches and individual members lose the vision and passion and motivation that drove them to do "whatever it takes" to achieve their goals or mission. They begin to get lazy, to coast, to take for granted, to rest on their laurels, to refuse to change, to feel they can do no wrong, to quit caring. They become . . . complacent.

Ancient Israel did it. Many parts of Israel 2 today are doing it again. Yes, the cliché is true: Those who forget history are doomed to repeat it. We've heard it too: We have nothing to fear for the future but forgetting how God has led us.

First love is ecstatic. But unless carefully tended from both sides—unless made the highest priority—it can slowly die into embers. The "forever love" becomes only temporary. That's true not just of human relationships but of our connection with the One who made us.

Is the church complacent? In some ways and places, perhaps yes. But the far more important question is: In my relationship with God, *am I complacent?*

VIII. EVERYONE HAS A STORY
—Here Are a Few

AMAZING HAL—AND NORMA

I found this on the AP daily wire. What a contrast to the daily news of greed! I'm dropping in the story here just as AP reported it:

"MEDIA, Pa. (AP)—Travel company operator Hal Taussig buys his clothes from thrift shops, resoles his shoes, and reads magazines for free at the public library.

"The 83-year-old founder of Untours also gives away all of his company's profits to help the poor—more than $5 million since 1999. He is content to live on Social Security.

"Taussig takes a salary of $6,000 a year from his firm, but doesn't keep it. It goes to a foundation that channels his company's profits to worthy causes in the form of low-interest loans. (About seven years ago, the IRS forced him to take a paycheck, he said, because they thought he was trying to avoid paying taxes by working for free.)

"If he has money left at the end of the month in his personal bank account, he donates it.

"At a time of the year when many people are asked to give to the poor, Taussig provides a model for year-round giving.

"'I could live a very rich life on very little money. My life is richer than most rich people's lives,' said Taussig. 'I can really do something for humanity.'

"His decision to give away his wealth stems from a moment of clarity and freedom he felt when he wrote a $20,000 check—all of his money back in the 1980s—to a former landlord to buy the house they were renting. It didn't work out, but the exhilaration of not being encumbered by money stuck with him.

"'It was kind of an epiphany,' he said. 'This is where my destiny is. This is what I was meant to be.'

"He and his wife, Norma, live simply, in a country house in suburban Philadelphia that's nearly a century old, with two bedrooms and 2 1/2 baths. It is neither luxurious nor sparse, but a comfortable home filled with photos and knickknacks with wraparound views of trees and clothes drying on a clothes line. To cut energy use and help the environment, they don't own a dryer.

"Norma Taussig uses a wheelchair after suffering a stroke years ago. They have been married for 61 years and have three children, five grandkids, and five great-grandchildren.

"Taussig said his marriage improved when he and his wife decided in the 1970s to keep separate bank accounts. His wife lives on Social Security and savings from her job as a school district secretary and later as an employee of Untours travel. Her salary never went above $30,000 a year.

"Taussig said the house—purchased for $41,000 in 1986 and owned by his wife—is paid for, and so is her 12-year-old Toyota Corolla. Taussig has his bike for transportation, which he faithfully rides to and from work every day, three miles round-trip.

"He calls consumerism a 'social evil' and 'corrupting to our humanity' because of what he said is the false notion that having more things leads to a richer life.

"'Quality of life is not the same as standard of living,' he said. 'I couldn't afford [to buy] a car, but I learned it's more fun and better for your health to ride a bike. I felt I was raising my quality of life while lowering my standard of living.'

"Ben Cohen, cofounder of Ben & Jerry's ice cream, met Taussig through a network of social-minded businesses and describes him as 'a humble guy—not your typical CEO.'

"While big corporations give away more money than Taussig, Cohen said, the donation could be 'one-half of 1 percent of profits while Hal gave away $5 million, and that's 100 percent of his profits.'

"In 1999 Untours won the $250,000 Newman's Own/George Award for corporate philanthropy, given by actor Paul Newman and the late John F. Kennedy, Jr., publisher of the now-defunct *George* magazine. The awards event was held in New York City, but Taussig balked at paying the city's high hotel prices. He stayed at a youth hostel while he donated the quarter-million-dollar award to his foundation.

"Kennedy's reaction to his hostel stay? 'He stared at me blankly,' Taussig said.

"The Untours Foundation loans money to groups or businesses at around the inflation rate. The current loan rate is 3.7 percent. The foundation's tax filing shows total assets of $1.8 million in 2005, the latest record available, of which $1.6 million went to 38 groups or firms. Hal Taussig is the president, and his wife is the vice president. They don't get salaries.

"'I try to make the poor into capitalists,' Taussig said. 'They should be self-sustaining. You give them money and they run out and you have to give more. But if you give them a way to make a living, it's like teaching them how to fish rather than giving them fish.'"

—*AP story by Deborah Yao*

LAY DOWN THE GAVEL

Like everyone else, I followed the gripping case of 4-year-old Madeleine McCann, who disappeared a few years back in Portugal, where her British family was on vacation.

Police in Portugal at first named Madeleine's parents—Kate and Gerry—as suspects, based on controversial evidence. In time, the judicial system cleared the parents of suspicion—at least legally. But once accused, the suspicion would linger in some minds.

It's happened before.

Back in 1980, Seventh-day Adventist former pastor Michael Chamberlain and his then-wife Lindy were vacationing at Ayers Rock in Australia with their three children. Sometime during the night, the Chamberlains said, their 2-month-old daughter Azaria was dragged from a tent by a dingo.

Lindy was tried, convicted in 1982 of Azaria's murder, and sentenced to life in prison. On the basis of new evidence bringing forth reasonable doubt as to her guilt, her conviction was overturned in 1988. The Chamberlains' story was told in a 1988 movie starring Meryl Streep and Sam Neill entitled *A Cry in the Dark*. The Chamberlains' marriage became just one casualty of the enormous stress.

In December of 1996, 6-year-old child beauty queen JonBenét Ramsey was found murdered in the basement of her parents' home in Boulder, Colorado. With contradictory evidence, a grand jury failed to indict the Ramseys. JonBenét's mother, Patsy, died of cancer in 2006 at the age of 49, before the courts would later officially clear her of suspicion.

I've had my own experience in life with being judged—and in the minds of some, convicted—of things I've not done. Perhaps you have too.

My appeal is that we each try to remember the following:

• As Christians, especially, we've been counseled that generally speaking, it's best to lay down the gavel and steer clear of the judging business: *"Judge not,* and you shall not be judged. Condemn not, and you shall not be condemned. Forgive, and you will be forgiven"* (Luke 6:37, NKJV).

• But in some instances it's important that we do make a determination. In such cases, may I appeal that we grant to each other at least what the courts of our land provide—no prejudging; hearing out with fairness the evidence of both sides; and reaching a decision based on the weight of clear evidence?

• Only God truly knows all things. Human judgments are faulty at best. The guilty sometimes go free. The innocent sometimes are convicted. That being true, should we ever *rush* to a decision? Should we ever reach one before we've heard and evaluated *all* available evidence? And above all, should we ever join the mob of self-appointed judges in the illegitimate "court of public opinion" in trying and convicting anyone even before the true justice system has done its work?

• Perhaps most to be desired would be that somehow Christians and the church hold to an even higher standard of fairness in the application of justice than do the courts of the land. Unfortunately, my own experience tells me that the reverse can too often be true.

In some highly publicized cases, we may or may not ever know for certain the truth about guilt or innocence. But until or unless clear evidence or even proof surfaces, let's do the decent, honorable, and Christian thing: Grant the suspected or accused the presumption of innocence.

CONSIDER THE POSSABILITIES

TV Commercials for Overstock.com for quite some time featured a female spokesperson in a nearly all-white environment. One day, I noticed that a new spokesperson appeared—a young woman sitting on a sofa while extolling the advantages of shopping at Overstock.

While I noticed the change of spokespersons—the first was a brunet, and the new one was blond—I didn't give it any thought beyond that, until I ran across an article recently about the new spokesperson, Briana Walker.

In 2002 then-23-year-old Briana, an aspiring dancer, fainted in her car while driving to church on a southern California freeway at 75 miles per hour. Her car crashed into the divider, then spun like a top into the ditch by the highway. Her back was broken completely in half—she would never walk again.

In the years since, she has refused to let her disability limit her, though confined (a word she has utterly redefined) to a wheelchair. Strapping herself to someone else, she has plunged into space in a bungee jump. She strapped herself to another guy and jumped out of a plane. She lay on a surfboard and challenged the waves. She sat on another board and water-skied. She's gone skiing. And in her wheelchair, she has competed in triathlons and marathons.

Briana shares her story in her recent book: *Dance Anyway.*

"Yes, ironically, my last name is Walker," she laughs. "I'm thinking of changing it to Wheeler."

She was featured in a story that appeared in the fall 2006 issue of the Loma Linda University *SCOPE* magazine. The Loma Linda University Orthopaedic and Rehabilitation Institute developed PossAbilities, a community outreach program for people with disabilities.

"PossAbilities encouraged me to race," Briana says. Her first triathlon was a 2004 PossAbilities race.

Briana's dad, Ed, who calls his effervescent daughter "Little Sparkle," feared when the accident happened that his little sparkle's sparkle might go out forever.

"How could I have ever thought that?" he asks. "It's brighter than it's ever been."

The stories I most enjoy in this life are about people who have demonstrated something God seems to have built into us—the ability (subject, of course, to our choice) to overcome huge obstacles, setbacks, and cruel turns of fate—and rise above them.

Think about your own limitations—whether real or only apparent—and reflect on how often we needlessly add "im" to the beginning of the word *possible* and the letter "t" at the end of *can.*

STORIES FOR HEAVEN'S CAMPFIRE

James E. Appel, M.D., is a young 2000 graduate of the Loma Linda University School of Medicine, who says he went to medical school "for the sole purpose of doing missionary work."

His blog of a frontline medical missionary doctor's life in Africa is inspiring and moving—and as utterly real as blogging gets. As medical director of the Beré Adventist Hospital in a remote area of Chad (sometimes spelled Tchad) in central Africa, Dr. Appel's blogposts bring one face to face with the poverty and pathos of our fellow human beings locked into a life few of us can even imagine.

The hospital has electricity only four to five hours a day by a generator, and no phone service. Beré has 60,000 people, most of whom, Dr. Appel says, "live in mud huts and barely survive through subsistence farming of rice, millet, and peanuts." Temperatures can reach 130°F, but at least there's air-conditioning in the surgery area.

"I wanted to go to a place where no one else wanted to go," Dr. Appel says. "I wanted to fill a need there that no one else wanted to fill."

Sarah Andersen, from Denmark, had been working as a volunteer nurse at Beré for several months when Dr. Appel arrived in early 2004. They soon married. Of their work there, Sarah says, "We've been in many hopeless situations that make me long even more for heaven—make me see that suffering was not a part of God's plan."

I found personal inspiration in some of the remarks of this dedicated young couple:

"Only the person who takes risks is truly free."—Sarah.

"I want to look back on my life here on this earth and feel like I've done something worthwhile that can be told around the campfire in heaven."—James.

As a young man in college, I was challenged by the life of the late Dr. Jack Provonsha of Loma Linda, who was both an ordained minister and a medical doctor. That dual ministry inspired me to take both a theology major and premed. But besides wanting to be a preacher and a doctor, I also had dreamed from the age of 15 of being a writer and editor. One lifetime hasn't been enough to do everything. I did become a pastor and then for most of my career, a writer and editor—but ultimately could not accommodate medical school as well.

But Dr. Appel and his wife are living out the life of medical mission service that I still wish I had another lifetime to pursue. Though I've never met them and may not till around heaven's campfire, I can't even begin to say how much I admire the commitment and sacrifice of James and Sarah Appel.

HE SOLD HIS SOUL ON EBAY

Back in February of 2006 atheist Hemant Mehta ran an ad on eBay auctioning off a chance to save his soul. For each $10 of the final bid, Hemant promised to attend an hour of church services.

"I don't take my nonbelief lightly," he wrote in his ad. "However, while I don't believe in God, I firmly believe I would immediately change those views if presented with evidence to the contrary. And at 22, this is possibly the best chance anyone has of changing me."

Forty-one bids later the winning bid of $504 came in from Jim Henderson, a 58-year-old former pastor from Seattle, Washington.

Soon after the auction closed, Henderson flew to Chicago to meet Mehta. When they met in a bar, they sealed a deal a bit different from the one that math student Mehta had posted.

Instead of the 50 hours of Mehta attending church that Henderson was entitled to for his $504, Henderson instead asked Mehta to attend a dozen or so services at churches of Henderson's choosing and then write a report on what he found.

"I'm not trying to convert you," Henderson told Hemant. "You're going there almost like a critic. . . . If you happen to get converted, that's off the clock."

The churches included then-pastor Ted Haggard's New Life Fellowship in Colorado, Bill Hybel's Willow Brook Community Church in Illinois, and Joel Osteen's Lakewood Church in Texas.

Hemant eventually wrote the results of his unusual assignment in a book entitled *I Sold My Soul on eBay.*

The book is a fascinating glimpse of Christianity and its churches through the eyes of a nonbeliever. It's a mirror held up to Christians reflecting to them how they are seen and perceived by perhaps many of those they hope to win. Think "Mystery Shopper goes to church."

Mehta's report is in no way hostile, and he considers himself a "friendly atheist." In his visits he was sometimes almost too observant, noting that he was puzzled by the lack of real community in churches—families sitting far apart from other families. He also noticed how Christians "raced out the front doors to their cars" immediately after the church service ended.

He found it odd how Christians seemed OK with singing what to him were exceptionally repetitive songs—and how they referred to non-Christians as "lost."

So far, no church has won Mehta over. But then, it's really God who, through the Holy Spirit, wins people—sometimes through, and sometimes in spite of, the efforts of Christians. And I'm confident God will be on his case 24/7.

Meanwhile, we Christians could do worse than to let God take care of Hemant and focus our attention instead on how we come across to nonbelievers.

IX. SONGS FOR
My Days—and Nights

BLESSING IN THE THORN

"Life is difficult."—M. Scott Peck, *The Road Less Traveled*

"Man . . . is of few days, and full of trouble."—*Job 14:1*

"In the world you will have tribulation."— *John 16:33, NKJV*

Yes, life *is* hard. It's difficult. It's full of trials and problems and tribulation. Not always, of course, but often enough. And sometimes it's more than difficult—it's overwhelming and seems unbearable.

Until the great battle between good and evil is over, no one can promise you a rose garden, a bed of roses, or even a dozen long-stemmed red roses.

But you and I have a choice. We can either choose to lament that roses have thorns, or we can choose to be grateful that thorns have roses. The thorns of tough times in our lives are always accompanied by roses of blessing. And we'll find them when we learn where to look.

A few years ago a great blessing came into my life. I was diagnosed with cancer. Yes, the thorns were sharp and painful: four surgeries in two years, chemo, radiation, great personal loss, physical and emotional wounds that would take much time to heal. But in the thorn was also great blessing. I emerged from that battle with my priorities reordered, with a new appreciation for the golden value of each moment of life, and with a stronger faith in my Creator.

Some days, too weak even to move and fighting to ride out pain that even medications could not fully control, I clung to the message of a song that I would play over and over. Some nights, feeling utterly alone and fearing I might not survive to see another morning, I was comforted by the song's assurance that even in the midst of a raging personal storm, God was there with me—I was not alone.

The thorn of cancer did indeed contain a blessing. Many blessings, actually. Not in an eternity would I have chosen to experience cancer. But when it came, I felt not only the deep wound of its thorn but the deep blessing of its power to transform me in ways profound, needed, and many.

As you read these words, I'm keenly aware that you too know what it is to encounter tough times in life. Perhaps you're in the midst of one right now—a trial that threatens to overwhelm or even destroy you.

Maybe you are wrestling with financial problems that seem too large to solve. Maybe you're seeing—or have already—the ending of your marriage. Perhaps you're trapped in a dark void of grief or depression. Or perhaps you too face a frightening health crisis.

Tough times invade every area of our lives. We can't escape them. But we can learn how to get through them to the other side. We can learn how to hang on to our faith and our sanity even when the winds of trouble scream through our lives with hurricane-force destructive power. We can learn how to survive—to discover that dark clouds *do* have silver linings—and that thorns too have roses.

IT IS WELL

It had been one of his favorite songs. Even as a boy I'd heard him singing it in his baritone-bass voice. So as I grew from childhood to manhood I'd found myself occasionally singing it too—nearly always when I was quite sure no one could overhear me!

Though I'm only minimally gifted musically, I love this special language of music that expresses so much that nothing else can. And through the years certain songs or compositions have come to have special and profound meaning—they express what lies too deep inside for words.

The favorite of my dad's to which I've alluded is entitled "It Is Well With My Soul." So it seemed only right that the day we said goodbye to him on September 11—the same morning the twin towers fell—that this song would be part of that goodbye.

Somehow she made it through the words, her voice bravely holding strong. My daughter Lorna stood next to the flag-draped casket of her grandfather (Dad was a World War II veteran), and one of those to whom I had passed on life filled the autumn air with the song so often sung by one who had passed life on to me.

I'm convinced that if I could truly keep the words of this song in mind more frequently, I'd know that "whatever my lot," all is well with my soul!

When peace, like a river, attendeth my way,
When sorrows like sea billows roll—

Whatever my lot, Thou has taught me to say,
It is well, it is well with my soul.
It is well with my soul,
It is well with my soul,
It is well, it is well with my soul.

Though Satan should buffet, though trials should come,
Let this blest assurance control,
That Christ hath regarded my helpless estate,
And hath shed His own blood for my soul.
It is well with my soul,
It is well with my soul,
It is well, it is well with my soul.

My sin—O the joy of this glorious thought—
My sin, not in part, but the whole,
Is nailed to the cross, and I bear it no more:
Praise the Lord, praise the Lord, O my soul!
It is well with my soul,
It is well with my soul,
It is well, it is well with my soul.

And, Lord, haste the day when my faith shall be sight,
The clouds be rolled back as a scroll:
The trump shall resound and the Lord shall descend,
"Even so," it is well with my soul.
It is well with my soul,
It is well with my soul,
It is well, it is well with my soul.

NO MORE NIGHT

My reading friend ... are you experiencing right now your own "dark night of the soul"? Are you ... or is someone near and dear to you ... battling cancer or some other life-threatening disease? Have you recently stood at the graveside of someone you love, saying a heartbreaking goodbye?

Then today I have for you some Bible verses and a song to recommend. First, listen to this from Revelation 21:1-4 and 22:5 in the New Living Translation:

"Then I saw a new heaven and a new earth, for the old heaven and the old earth had disappeared. And the sea was also gone. And I saw the holy city, the new Jerusalem, coming down from God out of heaven like a beautiful bride prepared for her husband. I heard a loud shout from the throne, saying, 'Look, the home of God is now among his people! He will live with them, and they will be his people. God himself will be with them. He will remove all of their sorrows, and there will be **no more death or sorrow or crying or pain**. *For the old world and its evils are gone forever.'" "And there will be* **no night there**—*no need for lamps or sun—for the Lord God will shine on them. And they will reign forever and ever."*

The song is one that has helped me through some of my own truly dark valleys. I first heard "No More Night" as sung by Jennifer LaMountain—and later enjoyed its rendition by the amazing tenor David Phelps, for several recent years a part of the Gaither Vocal Band.

Let me highly recommend you go to YouTube and enter the song title or "David Phelps." Then let the music bless and speak to you. I assure you that afterward, whatever your burden, it will be lighter.

THE OTHER SIDE

No piece of music means more to me. Of course, I'm not alone in that—the orchestral work to which I refer was voted in a recent poll to be the single most powerful piece of music ever written.

I don't want in this book to refer too often to my struggle a few years ago with cancer. But as anyone who has done so can tell you, battling this dragon is a profound and life-altering experience. One night I pretty much hit bottom. I so wanted out—just wanted to take a little more morphine than my prescribed allotment—and gradually drift into a final merciful sleep.

But as I lay there in only partially masked pain—without hair, alone, and almost too weak to think from a chemo dose my oncologist said was the largest he'd ever given—I pulled on my headphones and placed in the player Samuel Barber's *Adagio for Strings,* Opus 11, played by the New York Philharmonic, with Leonard Bernstein conducting. I closed my eyes and let the mournful, haunting music flow over me.

I played it several times, and somehow the feelings of oppressive sadness and hopelessness began to dissipate. As the *Adagio* climbed ever so slowly and inexorably to a soaring summit, followed by a quiet denouement, I truly felt as if I were being transported to a hilltop bathed in light, where I could look over if only briefly and see "the other side"—the place I want to spend eternity. It was for me a singularly sublime moment. And in the final quiet moments of the *Adagio,* it's as if I heard—as clearly as ever I have—God assuring me that all would be well.

When Arturo Toscanini first performed the *Adagio* in 1938 (two years after Barber had composed it at the age of 26), the audience was stunned. Many were even moved to tears—as I had been that lonely and dark night of my soul—yet after long moments of silence, a standing ovation followed. The composition shook the music world.

In the years to come the poignant *Adagio* would prove its power to reach people in all walks of life. In 1945 it was played at the funeral of Franklin D. Roosevelt—and in 1963 on the death of John F. Kennedy—as well as on the passings of Princess Grace and Prince Rainier of Monaco and Princess Diana. It was famously used in the Vietnam cinematic epic *Platoon,* as well as in several other movies (including *The Elephant Man, The Scarlet Letter, Lorenzo's Oil,* and *Amélie*).

On September 15, 2001, the *Adagio* was performed as a memorial to the victims of September 11 four days earlier, by the BBC Orchestra, magnificently conducted by Leonard Slatkin, in London's Royal Albert Hall.

As the twin towers fell, that same morning I sat—on the other end of the nation—at the graveside service for my father. How I miss him! During my illness he had changed my dressings, stayed whole nights in my hospital room, and cared for me—his only and namesake son—in my nearly helpless state as he had decades earlier in my childhood. I so look forward now, with yearnings too deep for words, to seeing him and my other Father on the other side—previewed for me in the powerfully moving *Adagio.*

X. THE SOVEREIGN
Power of Choice

OVERCHOICE, PRIORITIES, AND FILTERS

All the way back in 1970 (and stay with me here, you younger whippersnappers . . . even an old geezer might have something worth saying) I ran into one of the books that would make a lifelong impact on me: *Future Shock*, by Alvin Toffler.

In his seminal analysis of societal change, Toffler spoke of the accelerating pace of life, of the "dizzying disorientation brought on by the premature arrival of the future," and a phenomenon for which he coined a new word: *overchoice.*

As a kid, I remember the corner market in my town. The items—and their prices—rarely changed, and I could easily find anything in the store. Even the "big" store—the local Safeway—in my day had about 10,000 items.

Today I walk into a "superstore" and need a map to find anything in the acres of "stuff" stretching to the horizon. The average supermarket now stocks more than 45,000 items. A Walmart Supercenter can carry more than 100,000 items.

Want more? Consider the Internet. More than 433 million Web sites offering 15 billion pages.

Overchoice.

TV, radio, newspapers, magazines, the Internet, the superstore, and every other store in your town—they are all after two things that you and I have: *attention* . . . and a *decision.*

And every new day we wake up to spend our hours being bombarded with an endless cacophony of ads, commercials, pitches, appeals, enticements, and offers—every last one of them competing for your *attention* and mine.

The voices that snag our attention then try to push our buttons so that we'll *decide* something, so that we'll *choose:* to buy, to give, to sign up, to join, to get involved, to donate, to say yes to love or no to drugs.

Overchoice.

Then, besides the unsolicited barrage of voices with an agenda, there's your life—and mine. Decisions to be made about big things like career and life companion and spiritual stance. Important things like finances and health and relationships. Necessary things like car maintenance and shopping to re-stock and trips to the bank and post office. Personal things like which TV programs to watch, what music to download, what clothes to wear today.

Your chooser getting tired yet?

Truth is, there's not a prayer that any of us can address every available choice in a day's time. So to survive overchoice without being overwhelmed, we are going to have to *prioritize* and *filter*. And I'll tell you something I've discovered: these two things don't just happen. They are the result of deliberate, focused thought, planning, and reflection.

Millions float downstream through their days, drifting willy-nilly at the whim of the most successful appeals to their power of choice. They choose, often without really knowing it, what's easy, what's most fun, what feels best, what brings the fastest gratification.

"This one thing I do," the apostle Paul wrote (more on this in a moment). Paul focused. He chose. He prioritized. He filtered. And he accomplished. He succeeded. His life mattered.

It's still early in the year. Consider taking a day—just one day—to get alone with a pen and pad, quietness, no cell phone or e-mail, and just your thoughts. Prioritize for this year. Apply the filters you'll use to automatically shut out certain voices.

Where will God fit into your life and your year? What changes will you choose to make and follow through till they're new habits? What voices will you give more attention? less?

A plaque on my college dorm room wall said: "Paul said, 'This one thing I do'—*not* 'These 40 things I dabble in.'" You and I are amazingly blessed with the sovereign power of choice. Let's choose to cut the dabbling, zero in on what matters, and transform life this year. It *can* be done!

HURTLING THROUGH THE NEXT 365

Ready or not, here comes the new year. Now, don't get all up in my face and tell me today isn't anywhere near January 1. Because the new year, for you and me too, begins with every new day.

Tomorrow morning begins the first day of the rest of your life. It can be the beginning of a whole new year for you. So even though you might not be in the habit of reviewing the past and previewing the future till the big globe falls in Times Square, why not take a few moments to consider your next 365 days on Planet Earth?

A year from now, will you and I be able to say that we've improved in our health, relationships, finances, and, perhaps most important, in our knowledge of God?

The 365 new pages that stretch ahead of us from now till a year from now are there for us to write on. And what we write is not beyond our control. Some small part of it may be, but most of it will be what we *choose* to write. The sovereign power of choice that God has given to each of us can transform our lives in ways so profound they are breathtaking.

So whether it's January 1, May 22, September 19, December 31, or some other day as you're reading these words, join me in the only resolution you'll ever really need:

Make Better Choices.

THE SKYWALK, MUD AND STARS, AND PETER

Less than a half day's drive from where I temporarily hang my hat, a new tourist attraction recently opened at the Grand Canyon in Arizona. Located on Hualapai Indian land, the Grand Canyon Skywalk is a horseshoe-shaped, heavily reinforced, glass-bottomed walkway extending 70 feet over the canyon edge, affording a view 4,000 feet down to the Colorado River.

Now, even though I'm relatively near to the Skywalk, if the final 14 miles of unpaved road to get there didn't cool my enthusiasm about visiting it, I'm sure the $75 per person fee and the prohibition against cameras definitely would. But then, I'm such a killjoy that I don't even like paying for amusement park rides to give myself the willies. I can scare the bejabbers out of myself for free just looking in the mirror right after I get up in the morning.

So what's my point here?

Where you choose to look makes all the difference.

I could go to the Skywalk, look 4,000 feet straight down, and "enjoy" the queasy vertigo and mild acrophobia—or I could stretch out on my back on a blanket in the nearby desert at night and look straight up light-years and be awe-inspired by the canopy of the night sky shimmering with the light of countless billions of stars.

Which reminds me of the old couplet:

> *"Two men look through the same prison bars—*
> *One sees mud; the other sees stars."*

Where you choose to look makes all the difference.

Ask Peter out there walking on the water. He looked back at his friends in the boat. He looked at the huge waves around him. Where he did *not* look was at Jesus. And Peter began to sink like a rock.

I've had the same problem at times. Instead of looking to Jesus, I've looked at the waves of trouble. Instead of looking toward solutions, I've focused on the problem. And when that happens, I too begin to sink like a rock into a black hole of discouragement and hopelessness.

Where you choose to look makes all the difference.

And the incredible thing is, you have within you the almighty, sovereign power of choice to *decide* where you look. So do I.

We can choose to throw ourselves pity parties and wail and "awful-ize" and play the victim role to the hilt. Or we can look up. We can focus on Jesus . . . on solutions . . . on the good things in our lives . . . on our blessings . . . and refuse to let the troubles and negativity in this world pull us down.

Yes, there's plenty of ugly, negative stuff in this world—and it invades our lives every single day. We can't avoid trouble and pain and stress and loss. But we *can* choose how to respond to it. Will we focus on the thorns— or on the roses? Will we curse our bad luck—or find the blessing in it? There is always, in the words of one of my favorite songs, a "blessing in the thorn."

You see, *where you choose to look makes all the difference.*

GOD'S THIRD-BEST GIFT

Some people you could leave alone for decades—and they'd never do it. Others—you turn your back for five minutes, and they've done it twice.

Some people fear it, while others embrace it.

Some people desperately want to but can't seem to make it happen. Others will do almost anything to keep it from happening.

But inevitably, time alone will bring at least some of it.

We're talking, of course, about . . . *change.*

I read a book some time ago called *What You Can Change and What You Can't.* True, some things you just can't change. Your age. Your birthplace. Your gender (well . . . some do try!). The past. Your parents. Your DNA.

But there's a lot you *can* change: things that are within your sovereign free will—your power of choice—to change. Your future doesn't have to be an extension of your past. You can change your attitudes, your beliefs, your friends, your body, your goals, your habits, your thoughts, and your responses to the bad things life brings.

Why can you change all these things? Because at least for the things you *can* change, change is a function of *choice.*

You can *choose*—or not—to love, to believe, to let others control or manipulate you, to be a victim, to be a people-pleaser, to start over new, to do the hard things, to create your own future, or to reach your full potential.

Now, some of these possibilities for change—especially behavioral ones—can be accomplished simply by combining desire with repeated choice translated into action. But some of them—the more "inner" and spiritual changes—can succeed only as God is involved. "For God is working in you, giving you the desire . . . and the power to do what pleases him" (Philippians 2:13, NLT).

Choice and change. Inseparably linked. And ultimately, the greatest power any of us has.

I'd rank free choice as perhaps God's third-best-ever gift—after life itself and salvation. So let's use it wisely today—but for sure, let's use it!

I'm going to use it right now to abandon my keyboard here and go take a walk and get some sunshine.

HAIR CONDITIONER AND MOVING MOUNTAINS

Somewhere in your life right now is a mountain. You have one—maybe more—and so do I. It's part of our humanity, part of being alive on Planet Earth.

Some of those mountains are the direct result of our own faulty choices. Some appeared in our life simply because we live in a sinful world.

Mountains?

Yes. Mountains of debt. Mountains of deeply entrenched habit. Mountains of "excess avoirdupois" (one of many euphemisms for *fat*). Mountains that rise between us and those we love. Mountains that stand squarely between us and our dreams.

Mountains?

But didn't Jesus Himself say, "If you have faith as a mustard seed, you will say to this mountain, 'Move from here to there,' and it will move; and nothing will be impossible for you" (Matthew 17:20, NKJV)?

So why do we wake up each new day and find the mountains still there? Could it be that we've read Christ's promise but misapplied it?

If you live long enough, you discover that just being a Christian doesn't give you the magical power of looking at the mountain in your front yard, snapping your fingers while intoning the mustard-seed promise, and *voilà*—the mountain instantly disappears.

Those with the unrealistic expectation that the outcome of faith and prayer is unfailingly a miracle are doomed to be disappointed—sometimes to the point of total disillusionment about faith and Christianity. On this very point some depart from the faith, to walk in it no more.

What, then, means the promise of Christ in Matthew?

The key is to understand that while God sometimes—for reasons we may not fully understand while here in this life—can perform outright, instantaneous miracles, that is not the way He *usually* works.

Instead, God's usual way of working is to turbocharge the gift He has already given us—the vastly underestimated yet staggeringly potent power of choice.

The mountain can be removed. But not typically with one mighty *macro*-choice. No, the mountain yields to 1,000 or 10,000 or 100,000 daily *micro*-choices.

Long ago I used to use a hair conditioner called Small Miracle. It's the best one I ever found. Unfortunately, they stopped making it. I guess not enough others had my opinion of it. The way to move mountains is through a persistent, continuing series of "small miracles"—small, incremental, daily/hourly choices.

I like to identify the "big" things I've learned. One of the biggest and most awesome is the stupendous power of steady, incremental choices.

You don't choose to lose 5, 10, 50, or 100 pounds. You choose for this day—this meal—not to eat some things, to eat others, and to eat less in total. You choose to become more active. And you keep making these choices day after day after day.

You don't choose to pay off all your debts in a week. You choose to chisel away at them one dollar, one small check, at a time.

You don't typically get well because you put all your faith in instant healing. You recommit to following the laws of good health, and you take advantage of the wisdom and skill God has made available through health-care professionals.

You don't learn a language all at once. You don't go to sleep one night with a spare tire and wake up with six-pack abs. You don't magically produce the relationship of your dreams in five days.

Any bad mountain worth removing—or even a good mountain worth creating where none exists—requires steady, stubborn, persistent, repeated choices. Inch by inch. Slice by slice. Step by step. Hour by hour.

Faith as of a mustard seed? To me, this speaks less of faith in the instant or sudden disappearance of the bad or appearance of the good at one's wish. Rather, it speaks of faith both in the possibility of a wonderful outcome through repeated good choices—and of God's cooperation with us in strengthening our will (power of choice) in whatever way He may.

I look at some circumstances of my life and fervently, devoutly, with the greatest longing, wish for a great miracle—for instant, massive change.

But I've learned that like the determined tortoise, I too can arrive at the finish line of my goals by focusing my faith on the inevitability of my arrival—and by choosing to take the "next step" toward my goal.

Great miracles will abound when Jesus returns: the resurrection, new bodies, immortality, eternity. Meanwhile I'll find great satisfaction and delight in the small miracles of incremental change that ultimately add up to a genuinely great miracle.

XI. BETTER
World Ahead

TOO MUCH WITH US

"The world is too much with us," wrote William Wordsworth.

Too much indeed—and too true, WW the poet. We do live most days looking through the wrong end of the telescope. The wrong end being our total preoccupation with two "worlds" to the exclusion of a third.

The first world that monopolizes our attention is the world revolving around "us." Our thoughts. Our feelings. Our hopes and worries, our dreams and fears. The minutiae of our successive days: the price of gas, the pile of bills, the never-shorter to-do list, that pain we've felt for two days now (something serious?), family and relationship concerns, the state of our walk with God. And so much more.

The second world is what we learn from the news about our home planet: global warming, never-ending war, political corruption and polarization, stories of individual violence—nearly always against the weak—that break our hearts, natural disasters, disease, and starvation. Basically, a world seemingly gone berserk.

Yet the third world only fleetingly enters our thoughts. The "world" beyond earth. The universe. Heaven. Any intelligent beings on other planets. And though we're here on earth for only 70 to 100 years or so, and though heaven and the new earth will be our home for billions and gazillions of years—life without end—we rarely seem to think of that waiting world.

Through one end of the telescope we see our daily routines and could assume from the media that nothing more important is going on in all the universe than what happens in Washington, D.C. Seen from God's end, what's happening in D.C. is small potatoes—relatively minor but long-foreseen developments in a far greater drama.

Remember those old hymns? "I'm a Pilgrim, and I'm a Stranger" and "I'm but a Stranger Here, Heaven Is My Home"? The way this world is shaping up, perhaps it would behoove us to spend less time fretting about the liberals and the conservatives . . . the flaws of the church . . . or even the drama of our personal daily lives . . . and let our minds look ahead to where we'll spend eternity. After all: "When we've been there ten thousand years, bright shining as the sun, we've no less days to sing God's praise, than when we'd first begun."

Somewhere out there is our God, who inhabits eternity, not time, and He knows and sees all that happens here on earth—all that happens in your thoughts and feelings, and mine. Could it be well worth our effort to try our best more often to see through His end of the telescope?

Yes, this world is too much with us—the next one, not enough.

WELCOME TO DYSTOPIA

As greatly to be desired as *utopia* might be, the fact is that before utopia, we're going to face *dystopia* instead. In a Christian frame of reference, this means that before heaven and an eternity of perfect happiness must come the rest of time here on earth.

Beliefs in Christianity differ on the arriving dystopia—the "time of trouble," the "tribulation," the last convulsions before the end of a planet that long ago became the playground of the forces of evil and their satanic leader.

Many maintain that before the worst of it, true believers will be spirited away in a "rapture" and be spared the final rage of the roaring lion who paces through earth, "seeking whom he may devour."

Others of us believe that even believers will stay put and live through the last horrific spasms of a dying world—the time the prophet Daniel foretold: "a time of trouble, such as never was since there was a nation even to that same time: and at that time thy people shall be delivered" (Daniel 12:1).

Bible prophecy envisions a time of unprecedented economic, social, and political turbulence—the arrival of dystopia, which various dictionaries define as a place where—and a time when—"life is extremely bad because of deprivation or oppression or terror," where "people lead dehumanized and fearful lives."

A place such as George Orwell envisioned in his prescient *1984*. A place of exponentially increasing violence, instability, danger, and yes, dry-mouthed fear. A place where everything seems in flux—and nothing seems solid anymore.

I'm not ready to commandeer a broadcast network and infuse alarm and panic into an already-deteriorating situation. But at the very least, this is no time to be apathetic and sleepy. Because every indication is that the final drama has already begun. It's time to be awake and aware—to *notice* what's happening around us and reference it to what the Bible has to say.

• When I see gas at megabucks a gallon and many food prices doubling,

I need to be awake to the possibility that the entire bottom could fall out of the economy we just take for granted.

• When I realize that the planet I live on is showing signs of the abuse we humans have inflicted on it, I need to stay awake to where this ends up, if we keep going without change.

• When I realize that some—even and perhaps especially Christians—wish to impose their legislated morality on everyone else, I can see how certain end-time prophecies could easily come to pass.

• When I feel all the moorings coming loose, notice the ever-more-violent tremors of finance and society and politics and human relationships and international wars and genocides, it sometimes feels as if I'm standing on the rumbling slopes of a Mount Saint Helens about to blow.

Dystopia has begun. Reach out for something and Someone solid to brace yourself. Stay awake. This is no time for the fatal denial of the ostrich response.

But do not lose heart. On the other side of the devil's last dystopian gasp *is* utopia!

ASTERISKS AND WHITEWASH

Sometime up ahead I'll be in the market for a new computer. So when Dell and Hewlett-Packard and others put their big ads in *USA Today* or on the Internet, I keep an eye on specs and pricing.

Often as not, you see a photo of a computer with keyboard, mouse, and a widescreen monitor. Price, let's say, is $999. Takes a bit of looking, but sure enough, there it is.

The asterisk.

Down below in the small print, you find that the monitor is "not included." There it is in the photo—with the price right beside it. But sorry, *you can't have* what's shown in the photo! For that, you have to fork over extra. What the headline promiseth, the asterisk taketh away—or sometimes, addeth on to the price.

* *"Not included" (whether monitors, batteries, or you name it).*
* *License, transfer, and documentation fees additional.*
* *Add state, federal, global, and galactic taxes.*

That's the way it goes here in our world. What you see is *not* what you get. There's always the asterisk. The hidden hook. The catch. The fine print. The strings attached.

Pharmaceutical commercials tout the wondrous, transformational miracles that the latest drug will work for you. Then they run by you about 15 seconds of mumbled, low-volume, hyperspeed side effects that typically need yet another drug to offset them.

Gas pumps say $3.99.9 a gallon. Why not just $4.00? Because, hey—if we keep it under four bucks, maybe people will think "Not so bad . . . just somewhere a bit over $3.00.

We for sure live in a what-you-see-is-not-what-you-get world. We're surrounded by lies and half-truths—some devious, some just little "white" ones. We operate far too often on the "whited sepulcher" principle Jesus opposed while here: whitewash on the outside—dead bones on the inside.

So we learn that naïveté is not in our best interest. True and fair enough. We do need to be aware and use the good sense God gave us in life. There's no virtue in being gullible. But what is to be lamented is that along with naïveté, we too often conclude that trusting is also not in our best interest. So we scrap it also and decide that the only way to deal with the asterisks is to become thoroughgoing, suspicious skeptics—even cynics.

So long as sin is alive and well, we may never get away from the sneaky, deceitful asterisks. But I really look forward to Life Part II, when sin is stone-cold dead and asterisks are too. I could really go for a world where what you see is *always* exactly what you get.

ARMAGEDDON, CHICKEN LITTLE, AND CRYING WOLF

One benefit of geezerhood (and AARP officially welcomed me into that fellowship a buncha years ago) is that you've lived long enough to develop some perspective. You can fit current events into a few decades of observation and draw comparisons.

With so much in our world misbehaving, some say Armageddon is just around the corner. Some say that Chicken Little was right—the sky *is* falling. And lots of little boys and girls are crying "Wolf!"

Admittedly, the world *does* at present seem to be "going to hell in a handbasket." And one of these days Armageddon *will* happen, the sky *will* fall, and the wolf *will* show up.

But as a geezer, I remember in my callow youth a decade when the same alarms were ringing. Rewind some 40 years, for example, to 1968. Only five years earlier JFK had been assassinated. In 1968, MLK, then RFK, met the same fate. Racial strife turned cities into bonfires. College campuses roiled in protest against the Vietnam War. Surely the end of the planet must be near!

A few years later Iran humiliated the United States by holding American hostages. Interest rates skyrocketed to more than 20 percent. (I remember well, as I had to get a mortgage at those loan-shark levels!) Gas prices spiked to a level that wouldn't be matched for more than 25 years. Surely the end of the planet must be near!

- Watergate.
- Iraq War I.
- September 11.
- Iraq War II.

And some say up next is a possible financial collapse—a new Great Depression.

Each major upheaval has sent preachers warning of Armageddon, pundits warning of worldwide catastrophe, and most of us into some level of fear and stress.

Is the world about to end? Is what we've seen lately evidence that indeed, "this is it"?

Maybe. Maybe not.

My own church rose out of a mid-1800s religious movement that set a date for the end of the world: October 22, 1844, to be precise. Obviously, that never happened. Yet scary world events still bring prophets out of the woodwork to proclaim a deadline for the end of human history.

My own church talks about the "great time of trouble" (see Daniel 12:1). Many other churches talk about the "tribulation." Some Christians believe in a "rapture" ahead of that dark time. Others of us believe in the return of Christ *afterward*.

So is this it?

You *could* make that case. Imminent economic collapse. The growing gulf between the haves and the have nots. Corruption and greed rampant. Terrorism seething and ready to explode. Endless war.

But given that other times have also loomed as scary and troublous in decades recently past, perhaps a bit of caution is in order. Perhaps we shouldn't reflexively join Chicken Little and the Boy Who Cried Wolf each time the sky darkens or we hear the faraway howl of a *Canis lupus*.

And perhaps above all, while it's good to keep one eye on world events and compare them to Bible prophecy, it's even better to be ready for the end of all things every single day we live. And that means centering our lives on Jesus—getting to know and trust Him better.

Far better, it seems to me, than monitoring world events to know just the right moment to start "getting ready" for the end of all things is *being ready* every day and staying that way! And being ready isn't trying hard to be good—it's trusting the One who *is* our only goodness.

Is this "the beginning of the end"? I don't know—and I don't think anyone can say for sure. One of these days the last events—the time of trouble—*will* take place. One of these days Jesus *will* return to end the misery and chaos. If this day's events are part of the process of getting from here to there, I say, "Bring it on!"

But if not—if time moves on another decade or two or four—I want to be sure *my* remaining time is spent peacefully developing my primary and eternal friendship, not in a constant panic of fear and stress as the world around me goes steadily more berserk.

BEES, ICE, AND A GROANING EARTH

Often as a kid I heard that the world would likely end at the second coming of Christ even before I could finish school.

Back in those happy days of the 1950s, the world was a vastly different place than it has now become. The imminence of the world's end was more an article of faith than a conclusion based on much real evidence.

Ironically, even as my church—weary of waiting—seems focused on many other things than the Second Advent, the evidence, for those with eyes to see, is growing from a trickle to a tsunami.

Romans 8 talks about the entire creation, the whole earth, groaning as it waits for deliverance at the return of Jesus. And the groaning, for those with ears to hear, is growing from a whisper to a whirlwind.

One week not long ago I read two stories that should cause, not panic, but sober realization that our remaining days on this dying planet are truly numbered.

Consider the bees. At least one reason world food prices, according to the World Bank, have risen by 83 percent in the past three years (surely at least *that* has been noticed) is the rapidly accelerating die-out of honeybees worldwide in a malady called colony collapse disorder (CCD).

Without the pollination of the bees, no food can grow. By 2008 beekeepers had lost a full 36 percent of their colonies. Albert Einstein once said that if the bees were to die out entirely, the human race would follow them to oblivion within four years.

Theorized causes for CCD range from pesticides and herbicides to cell phone waves, environmental contamination, and aggressive new parasites or pathogens.

But whatever the cause, no solution seems yet in sight, and as usual, nothing is likely to be done about it until, like our currently out-of-control gas prices, food prices too double, triple, and quadruple.

Consider also the polar ice cap. As I write this, scientists predict that this year for the first time in the memory and records of those alive today, the ice cap at the north pole is likely to melt away entirely.

Polar bears are in danger of extinction. World sea levels are rising. Strange weather extremes and anomalies are becoming commonplace. Some scoff that global warming is a myth—that it's a political invention. But for me, at least, ignoring solid scientific evidence is not just denial—it's self-destructive insanity.

Something *is* happening to the planet to cause melting ice caps and rising seas. To deny that much is to join with the flat-earthers and those who believe that the moon landings were filmed on a Hollywood back lot.

Bees. Ice. A groaning earth.

And all this leaves to be added—as signs of a world gasping its last—the raging violence and ethnic cleansing and terrorism of the world. It leaves to be added the steady abandonment of our Constitution and personal freedoms in the name of national security.

It leaves to be added the foul cesspool of societal norms and standards. It leaves to be added the increasing efforts of rigid religionists to legislate and compel from the outside rather than encourage transformation from the inside.

It would seem to me that we're witnessing such a rapid convergence of pre-Advent signs that it's no time to be apathetic, skeptical, or doubtful.

"In the last days there will be scoffers. . . . This will be their argument: 'Jesus promised to come back, did he? Then where is he?' " (2 Peter 3:3, 4, NLT).

Let's just be sure that the scoffers don't include *us*.

YEARNINGS

Sometimes I listen to a hauntingly beautiful melody, and it stirs something in me too deep for words—a longing desire for life always to be so beautiful, so uplifted, so pure, so calmly joyous.

Sometimes I experience human love so profound I'm taken to places I never realized could exist—and it's as if I'm previewing heaven.

Sometimes I grapple with the daily stresses and irritations of life and wish some days didn't have to be quite such a challenge.

Sometimes something surfaces from the center of my being, telling me that this isn't how it was meant to be—that we all were intended for something unimaginably better.

Sometimes I see through a glass darkly to glimpse something awesomely wonderful waiting on the other side. Here—only hints, shadows, and samples.

Sometimes I hear echoes of Eden unfallen—and the approaching Doppler waves of an impossibly perfect Eden restored.

XII. BELIEVING,
at Midnight, in Dawn's Sure Light

I HOPE

It was fun being young. Full of zeal and idealism and energy. Ready to plunge into life and apply all those years of learning: grade school, high school, college, grad school. Ready to chase dreams and make them happen. Ready to do something important if not amazing.

But growing older also has its satisfactions. Experience. Perspective. Wisdom. Lessons learned, not in classrooms, but through life's pains and pleasures, its failures and successes, its deep valleys and high mountaintops.

And as I'm growing officially "old" now by some arbitrary measures, I've come to discover by hard-won experience life's most important things. Love is king, of course. Family. Friends. Integrity. Perseverance.

But one of the most important virtues I've learned now to prize in life is . . . hope.

First Corinthians 13 speaks of "faith, hope, love, these three" (verse 13, NKJV). And while love gets top billing, I've learned that hope is often equally indispensable.

The Bible says that "we are saved by hope" (Romans 8:24). I've learned how utterly true that is.

We simply can't live without hope. Hope keeps you getting out of bed in the morning. Hope drives you to keep trying, even when it seems futile. Hope is the song you sing in the blackness of your personal midnight. Hope keeps the dying alive and the living energized.

Once we lose all hope, we're finished. Hopelessness is lethal. The will goes home. Possibilities die. Dreams crumble to dust. No more reason to *be* can be found.

In *The Shawshank Redemption*, Andy Dufresne wrote to his friend Red: "Remember, Red, hope is a good thing—maybe the best of things." Later in the story, as Red goes searching for his friend Andy, he says to himself:

> *I hope I can make it across the border.*
> *I hope to see my friend and shake his hand.*

I hope the Pacific is as blue as it has been in my dreams.
I hope.

Even though I'm older now, I too still hope:

I hope I get to enjoy my children and grandchildren for many more years.

I hope I can give love as generously as I've received it.

I hope to make a positive difference while I'm here, to as many as possible.

I hope to become less flawed and selfish and more like Jesus.

I hope the blessed hope will be soon.

I hope to see all those I love on "the other side."

I hope you are there too.

I hope.

TAKING THE STING OUT OF DEATH

Back in my academy English classes, I remember my first real introduction to the works of the great poets. Among others . . .

The English-Scottish-Irish: Keats, Shelley, Coleridge, Donne, Wordsworth, Yeats, Burns, Milton, Kipling, Chaucer, Browning, Tennyson, and, of course, Shakespeare.

The American: Whitman, Longfellow, Dickinson, Thoreau, Millay, Eliot, and Frost—even Guest.

Once formal education is finished, life really sets in. It gets mighty hard to find time to read and enjoy poetry. And that's a shame. Because some of the greatest thoughts and emotions ever expressed are found in the works of history's creative scribes.

Take, for example, the words of John Donne (1572-1631), who, before he was 10 years old, lost to death his father and three of his sisters. Later in his life, in 1617, his beloved wife, Anne, died five days after giving birth to a stillborn baby. John mourned her deeply and never remarried. Grief-stricken, he wrote one of his most famous sonnets, in which he not only challenged the cruel enemy that had snatched away his wife but expressed his firm hope in death's ultimate defeat:

> *Death be not proud, though some have called thee*
> *Mighty and dreadful, for thou art not so . . .*
> *One short sleep past, we wake eternally,*
> *And death shall be no more; death, thou shalt die.*

If anyone cares to keep track of it, I'd like that chiseled into my own headstone if I don't last till the Second Coming.

In these words Donne echoed what Paul had already written centuries earlier:

> *"And the last enemy to be destroyed is death."*
> *"O death, where is your victory?*
> *O death, where is your sting?"*
> *—1 Corinthians 15:26, 55, NLT*

If you're still young, you may not think much about death. Trust me, though, time is going to pass far more quickly than you can possibly imagine—and soon enough you'll be in the shoes of some of us who have walked the trail of life ahead of you. Then you'll think increasingly of death, as first your grandparents, then your parents reach life's end—and you read the obituaries of former classmates, workmates, and friends.

But back to Paul and John (the pre-Beatle ones). After mowing down every generation from Adam till now, death is a hollow tiger—a doomed enemy. Yes, it's heartbreaking to say goodbye to those we love. But for those of us who cling to the only One ever to defeat death, we have the certainty of resurrection and reunion.

Mighty and dreadful? Donne asked of death. Hardly! he scoffed. Just a short sleep, and we wake eternally. You, death, on the other hand—you are the one who will die and never wake up! For those of us who trust in Jesus, death is for sure a comma, not a period—a pause, not a final end.

Death can seem so frightening—so formidable and intimidating, so powerful. But it's really a paper tiger, a snake without fangs, a scorpion with no sting.

Donne wrote from no ivory tower, but from the depths of his own sorrow . . . but also from the heights of his hope.

Not so far from where I live is Death Valley. From the lowest point in North America, you can look west and see the highest peak in the continental United States. If any of you are in the valley of the shadow of death, look up. Lift up your eyes to the hills, from which you can find hope—the hope of life resumed and never-ending.

Death will die. We will live! Thanks for that reminder, Paul and John.

LESSONS FROM A DESERT ISLAND

The year was 2000. I was still working my way out of a long tunnel of cancer treatment: surgeries, chemo, and radiation.

A movie came out that year—one that inspired me enough that I had to purchase it to view again—which by now I've done many times.

One line in particular seemed to sum up a word that had helped me get through the worst of it. A word that has surfaced again in this election year. The word? *Hope.*

You can survive almost anything as long as hope remains. When that runs out, all is lost. That's why I bought *Cast Away*—the story of a man stranded on a desert island who survived with ingenuity and hope.

The line that I found so helpful that I printed it out to post on my office bulletin board? "I know what I have to do now," Hanks' character said. "I gotta keep breathing. *Because tomorrow the sun will rise. Who knows what the tide could bring?"*

No matter how dark things look today, tomorrow is a new day. And as tomorrow's tide rolls in, you just never know what it could bring to your feet. So hold tight to hope.

New chances. Healing of body or heart. A fresh start. New love. Success to offset a failure. A sweet serendipity. Unexpected blessings. A small miracle or a life-changing event.

With tomorrow's rising sun, with tomorrow's incoming tide, you just never know!

SEEING JESUS

These next few words I may be unable to write without a few tears.

Let me begin when, as a young pastoral intern fresh out of the seminary, I stood in the pulpit of the Dallas First Seventh-day Adventist Church at 4009 North Central Expressway, for my first sermon in the "big" church. (I also had responsibility for the "satellite" church in suburban Mesquite, Texas.)

There on the pulpit, where only the speaker could see it, was a printed banner with the words, "Sir, We Would See Jesus" (quoting the words of the Greeks who lodged this request with Philip in John 12:21).

Perfect counsel for any preacher about to open the Word. And those words would become my benchmark for all the future times someone called on me to preach.

More than 30 years later I sat, on another September morning with my family, at the hospital bedside of my dying father. He'd struggled for some time with congestive heart failure—and a few days earlier had experienced a stroke. He was in a comatose state and nearing the end.

My family and I leaned in closely and whispered assurances of our love—and our hopes of seeing him soon in a better place.

"Dad, you're going to see Jesus soon," I told him.

Suddenly, his eyes—till then tightly closed—opened, and he seemed to be struggling to raise his head. Looking around at us, he gasped and echoed, "See Jesus! . . . See Jesus!" Then he lay back, closing his eyes again.

Soon after, he breathed his last. We gathered on an Idaho hillside four days later for his graveside service—while 2,500 miles east of us the twin towers fell.

Dad was a good man—flawed but decent and deeply committed to Jesus. I have no doubt that he will indeed soon "see Jesus." And I plan to be there when he does.

My first sermon at Dallas was on the Second Coming. Even so, come quickly, Lord!

XIII. THE
Supreme Gift

A GOD WITH SKIN ON HIM

Quite a few years ago, while pastoring a church in Albuquerque, New Mexico, I passed another church on the way to mine and noticed the words on their sign out front:

> *"Does God seem far away?*
> *Who do you think moved?"*

Sometimes we truly do feel as if God is far, far away. It can seem that He created this world and all of us—and then walked off like some absentee landlord to let us fend for ourselves.

But is it possible that if God seems far away, *He* is not the one who moved? Is it possible that sometimes we feel that way because *we* are the ones who have drifted away from Him?

The picture I get in reading the Bible is not of a remote, distant God, but of a Father who cares more about us than we may ever realize.

Perhaps you've heard the story by Christian author John Drescher about the frightened little boy who lay in his shadowy bedroom one night, trembling in terror as a thunderstorm raged just outside.

"Daddy," he called out, "please come here—I'm scared!"

"Son," his father answered, "it's OK—God loves you, and He'll take care of you."

"Yes, I know God loves me," the boy replied. "But right now I want somebody *who has skin on.*"

Each year when we celebrate the birth of Jesus perhaps we hear or read again those words in Matthew 1:23 in which Matthew quoted Isaiah's prediction of Christ's birth: " 'Behold, the virgin shall be with child, and bear a Son, and they shall call His name Immanuel,' which is translated, 'God with us' " (NKJV).

God *with* us. God nearby. God close at hand. God who cares about us more than any of us as parents care about our own children.

Some of us may be blessed to share this year's Christmas season with those we love. But some may spend this Christmas alone, or nearly so. Yet not really. Not if we realize that if God seems far away, He isn't the one who moved. Not if we realize that in Jesus we were given a God with "skin on"—the very word *incarnation* being based on the word for *flesh*.

The message of Christmas is that God is "with us." What's also wonderful to realize is that on awakening the morning of December 26, we discover that He is with us all the other 364 days of the year as well.

SEVEN WAYS TO SURVIVE CHRISTMAS

1. If you're old enough to read this, then remind yourself that you've done this before—and none of those Christmases Past finished you off.

2. Enough with the perfection already. You get to go on living even if you don't get everything done. And you're not auditioning to replace Martha Stewart, Oprah, or any other sentient being, human or divine.

3. Consider giving people gifts that don't need wrapping: cards redeemable for focused time with you or gifts that involve your talents or expertise. And for the kids (or even adults), some homemade items. Remember popcorn-string tree garlands? the homemade wooden truck your dad built for you? the dress your mom sewed for you?

4. Think minimal, think frugal, think downscale, think keep-it-simple. Think less of things and more of people—less of the clock and calendar, and more of those who have little or nothing.

5. Give of yourself and your means as much as you can, not only to those near and dear, but also to those also who have nothing to give back but their gratitude.

6. Refuse time stress, money stress, do-it-all stress. Slow down, smell the roses (or enjoy the poinsettias), ask for help, delegate, raid the Dollar Store. If you and your family were stranded on a desert island with only each other at Christmas, would you maybe enjoy each other—and Christmas—just as much?

7. It may be almost a cliché by now, but to belabor the obvious, try not to leave Christ out of Christmas. This day isn't about you or Santa Claus or Frosty or shopping till you drop. It's about Him. It's about love and giving—of which He's the source. It's about His creation and enjoyment of relationships. Include Him in—more than ever this year—and see what an amazing difference it makes!

THE BEST CHRISTMAS GIFT YOU CAN GIVE

Nearly 40 years ago now, singer/songwriter Harry Chapin wrote and sang a song that captured all too accurately how parents often fail to give their children the one gift they most want and need.

"Cat's and the Cradle" told the story of a father too busy to spend time with his young son. The father gave the little boy plenty of things—even one time, a new baseball. But when the lad wanted his dad to spend time playing ball together, the father begged off, saying that right now he was too busy, but that later they'd have a good time.

But later never came. And the years raced by. The young son grew up and had a family of his own. Now the tables turned, as the father, now retired, finally wanted to spend time with his grown son. By now, though, the son had duplicated his dad's busy life, and he begged off.

Chapin's song ends with the father realizing that his boy had grown up to be just like him—too busy, and with priorities out of whack.

Christmas will be here again soon enough. This Christmas, consider the gifts you plan to give to those you love.

Perhaps all of us could do well to remember that a gift that far surpasses anything else we could give is not something that fits under a tree. It won't fit in a box.

The greatest, most needed, most desired gift of all is to give ourselves—our time, our care, our undivided attention, our focused interest, our encouragement, our affirmation, our love.

For some this Christmas will reflect a prosperous year. For others it will be a "lean" Christmas—with little or nothing for gifts. But there's not a one of us who can't give the most treasured gift of all—ourselves.

Surprising Things Happen When You

Follow God

Here I Am, Lord—Send Someone Else

How I Ended Up in Africa

CURT DeWITT

When God called Curt DeWitt to be a missionary in Africa, Curt found himself fighting off spitting cobras, helping capture criminals, and spiritually wrestling with the powers of darkness. In this hilarious account of his African adventures Curt proves that ending up where you least expected can be more exciting and satisfying than you ever imagined.

Paperback, 156 pages.
978-0-8280-1942-2.